PARTICIPATORY DEMOCRACY

PARTICIPATORY DEMOCRACY:

Developing Ideals
of the Political Left

by
Daniel C. Kramer

SCHENKMAN PUBLISHING COMPANY
CAMBRIDGE, MASSACHUSETTS
Distributed by General Learning Press

Schenkman books are distributed by
General Learning Press
250 James Street
Morristown, New Jersey 07960

CONTENTS

CONTENTS

PREFACE

Whatever its substantive defects, this volume differs significantly from most recent works that can be considered as falling within that vague category which American scholars and book publishers call "histories of political ideas." The average historian of political ideas will devote a good deal of time to elucidating the meaning of the ideas with which he is concerned. He will also (if he is concerned with only one or two men) give a rather complete biography of his subjects and describe the interplay between vicissitudes in life and changes or modifications in viewpoint. Often there will be no attempt to evaluate the ideas: when there is one, it is almost always in terms of the internal consistency of the subjects' writings. The only time that a serious effort is made to adjudge these doctrines in the light of the real world is when, and to the extent that, these doctrines consist of predictions of things to come in the fairly near future. Writers such as Karl Marx are thus frequently exposed to criticism in the light of reality, though all too often on the part of both Marxists and anti-Marxists this criticism merely revolves about his assertion that free enterprise is on its deathbed, that capitalism means increasing misery for the proletariat, that international proletarian solidarity will soon replace lower-class jingoism, etc. But when and to the extent that a political writer did not try to foretell the shape of the future, his proposals are rarely tested for feasibility in the light of real institutions which are analogous to those whose establishment he favors. There is, in short, a wide gap between the student of political ideas on the one hand and the political universe of both his subjects and of himself on the other.

This book attempts to bridge that gap. We shall not

1

only attempt to explain a certain political theory popular today ("participatory democracy") and to show that this theory is not too different from that expounded by some socialist thinkers of the nineteenth century and the early part of this one, but shall also try to determine, looking to existing institutions such as factory works councils, university faculty departmental meetings, and elective boards that have a say in the operation of anti-poverty programs in slum areas in the United States, whether this theory would realize one of the major goals of those who are propounding it. This analysis will also help us answer the broader question of whether it is worthwhile striving for the implementation of this theory. (It is a departure from the approach of the average historian of political ideas merely to say that the question of whether the views of his thinkers are practicable is one that should be answered.)

This book originated from thoughts that began to keep me awake when I was writing my doctoral dissertation on the political and social thought of G. D. H. Cole. However, aside from its study of German and Yugoslav works councils and its few pages relating Cole to the current theory we shall be analyzing, it bears practically no resemblance to that dissertation. I would hope, however, that the readers of this book will be stimulated to read for themselves some of Cole's major works: he is a highly perceptive theorist who is, unfortunately, neglected at present.

Finally, it is enough justification for the publication of this work that it tests an idea that is in the process of becoming part of the left's standard stock of political wisdom. However, I think that its section of most permanent value is that in which it attempts to define and explain the concept of the "self-governing citizen." I have a hunch that the current call for "participatory democracy", including the creation of factory works councils and neighborhood governments, will become a bit less audible in the near future. However, until that horrendous day arrives when Strangelovian scientists develop a technique for altering a human embryo's genes to make him completely passive in the face of those who call themselves his rulers, many individuals will keep on demanding to be self-governing; and our discussion of when they can be called self-governing can serve as a standard to help them judge whether or not this claim has been satisfied. It is not that this test is the only one they can use; but it is, in my opinion, a reasonable one, and one cannot ask much more than that of a standard for judging a social situation.

The list of persons and institutions to thank for making it possible for me to write this book is so extensive that I can set forth only a small part of it here. I wish to thank Kenyon College, Gambier, Ohio, for arousing me from an adolescence of mental slumber; the much-abused U.S. government, for awarding me a Fulbright Fellowship to the London School of Economics; the University of Pennsylvania, for awarding me fellowships which made it financially feasible for me to attend graduate school; Raymond English, James C. Charlesworth, Jewell Cass Phillips, and Henry Abraham for an excellent education in political science; all the persons whose interviews with me have been used in the following pages; my in-laws Percy and Marjorie Lee; my parents Samuel and Mildred Kramer; my wife Richenda; and, most especially, my children Tamsyn, Elspeth and Bruce, without whom this book would, they insist, have appeared two years earlier. Incidentally, many of the above-named persons would disagree with most if not all of the ideas in this volume.

I

TODAY'S POLITICAL LEFT

Every age seems to have its left-wing battle cry. In 1776 the Virginian Patrick Henry demanded "Give me liberty or give me death." His call for the abolition of tyrannous monarchy found in the same years its economic counterpart in Adam Smith's supplication for laissez faire: give the businessman freedom to conduct his enterprise as he sees fit and an "invisible hand" will insure the greatest happiness of the greatest number. The French Revolution culminated, it is true, in an autocratic majoritarianism and then the Napoleonic dictatorship, but it held forth to the world the promise of the Rights of Man. This call for liberty, political and economic, can be said to have been the standard under which the forces of the left marched throughout much of the nineteenth century. The U.S. Civil War's "Battle Hymn of the Republic" urged the men in blue: "As He died to make men holy, let us die to make men free," and these lines could have been taken as the distillation of the political philosophy of men like Byron, Mazzini, Jefferson, O'Connell, the Chartists, etc.

But the economic freedom which men like Jefferson assumed went hand-in-glove with political liberty proved a sham for the masses of men in the Western world. They had full freedom to bargain with their employers, but what a mirage that prerogative proved to be. If the worker did not like the pittance he was receiving, he was legally free, it is true, to demand from his boss a sum sufficient to give him and his family a warm, decently ventilated habitation and

5

adequate clothing and food. But in practice he could not exercise this right, for he knew very well that if he did, the entrepreneur would simply replace him with one who had no work.

Even during the first half of the nineteenth century a minority of the left was aware of these problems and attributed them to the control of the economy by individuals motivated only by the wish to "accumulate, accumulate." This minority concluded that the capitalist hydra must be overthrown, or at least be subjected to some sort of regulation by the newly free people in their collective capacity, i.e., by the state. During the second half of that century, and even more during the twentieth, the left turned almost unanimously to the repudiation of laissez faire. To Marx and Engels, capitalism was not only evil but doomed, and would soon be eradicated in a working class revolution which would produce an economic system whose form was not too clearly defined but which would end the exploitation of man by man. The Fabian Socialist in Great Britain saw that the nineteenth century state itself was busying itself more and more with economic matters, and held that this process was bound to continue until the major means of production were under public control. In the United States of America first the Populists and then the Progressives demanded more state and national control of their particular villains: the railroads, the banks, the grasping magnates who paid their help a starvation wage but who considered themselves trustees whom a white, Anglo-Saxon, Christian God had commanded to provide for the welfare of the masses. In short, from "political freedom-laissez faire" the left's slogan became "abolish poverty by abolishing laissez faire": most of the left retained its devotion to political liberty but a few became so crazed by the glare from their collectivist Utopia that they developed the wish to annihilate all those who dared stand in their way.

After the first and second world wars, this new slogan of the left was partially achieved. Poverty was completely abolished almost nowhere, but laissez faire suffered a deathblow. In Russia and Eastern Europe the economy came under the total control of the central government; Great Britain and the Scandinavian countries were transformed into semi-socialist democracies with a significant amount of government ownership of business plus a full-fledged welfare state. In the United States there was very little nationalization but much acceptance, in both theory and practice, of the thesis that it is the duty of the state to insure the health of the economy and an adequate standard of living for all. Likewise, the government of West Germany acts in accordance with its assertion that "It is the State's first obligation to observe and to protect the dignity of man and thus to enable the individual to lead a life worth of man, insofar as that individual is unable to do so by himself."[1] So North America and Europe have followed the road to socialism or at least welfarism. Moreover, the newly liberated "Third World" has decided that there is no need for it to suffer even temporarily from the cruelties of the pure free enterprise system so beloved of Smith and Herbert Spencer. For example, the Preamble to the Indian Constitution proclaims the achievement of social and economic justice one of the Republic's primary purposes while its Article 19 (2) allows the state to impose reasonable restrictions on the right to hold property and to carry on a business; and the Indian national and state governments have made frequent use of this prerogative. In fact, the doctrine that the political system should control or manipulate the nation's economy in such a way that no one need worry about starvation and that everyone can work under satisfactory conditions has become so orthodox that it can be political suicide to advocate a return to pure laissez faire, as Barry Goldwater and his Republican Party discovered in the 1964 U.S. Presidential elections.

This being the case, we would expect that the left in the modern western world, at least, would feel rather close to the governments of the various western nations. It is true that a

Russian or Pole who genuinely loves political freedom would have good reason to loathe the rulers of his country, but freedom of speech, press, religion etc. is the rule rather than the exception in the United States, Great Britain, and France. One would accordingly predict that the left-wing Englishman, American or Frenchman would view his rulers as competent, honorable human beings who could, perhaps, go a bit faster in achieving the goals they mutually cherish. But in actuality, a significant minority of the left in the western world does at present view the political and economic structures of the several major western nations as antagonistic institutions which it is necessary to radically transform. This minority, which is overwhelmingly a youthful minority, is "alienated" from the state and from the society it dominates, in the sense that the society suspects and fears them and they suspect and fear it in turn. Witness the following incidents, which are doubtlessly familiar enough to anyone who read the *New York Times* with a fair degree of care during 1967-1968.

The then President of the United States, Lyndon Baines Johnson, was the man whose administration had succeeded in securing the passage of much legislation which the American left had been clamoring for in vain for at least two decades. A Civil Rights Act was passed in 1964 which made illegal racial and religious discrimination in most hotels, motels, restaurants, cinemas, businesses, and trade unions. A Voting Rights act enacted in 1965 was followed by a phenomenal increase in Negro voter registration in the southern United States. A Medicare bill relieved most of America's "senior citizens" of the fear of not being able to meet their often enormous medical and hospitalization expenses. And the Economic Opportunity Act of 1964 promised much in the way of curing the educational deficiencies from which the poorer third of the nation suffer and in providing them with the skills which they need in order to be able to hold a decent job. One not familiar with the American scene would suppose that Lyndon B. Johnson would have been the hero of U.S. progressives.

And yet the same Lyndon Baines Johnson was "immortalized" by the following doggerel chanted by many on the American left: "Hey, Hey, LBJ. How many kids did you kill today?" That same Lyndon Baines Johnson was so afraid of America's students that he arrived unannounced by helicopter in New York's Central Park for the funeral of a prominent American Catholic leader, was whisked off to St. Patrick's Cathedral, and then was spirited back to the Park for the return trip to the White House. His constituents, except for a few policemen, were kept unaware of his presence in the city until he had departed. His Secretary of State, Mr. Dean Rusk, a southerner who has left far behind the bigotry of his ancestors, was greeted in the same city by tomatoes thrown by youthful demonstrators. And, finally, Johnson was nearly beaten in the New Hampshire primary by a relative unknown in March, 1968, thanks to the immense amount of time and energy expended on behalf of his opponent by liberal and radical college students.

Many of those who expressed this opposition to Lyndon Baines Johnson also believe that the American university is itself a symbol of the hated political and economic system. This at first may seem strange, given the fact that the university is traditionally a non-profit institution devoted to the spread of knowledge and the creation of thinking human beings and that much of the more articulate faculty is itself emotionally and intellectually of the left. But there are obvious reasons for this identification — some of these institutions are financed by the states, others are managed by trustees dominated by businessmen, and a goodly number carry out "defense-related" research for the national governent (e.g., devote themselves to producing better instruments of biological warfare). And many of the better American universities have suffered from student rebellions which have gone byond the traditional liberal form of peaceful, albeit heated, verbal protest. University administration buildings have been seized, university presidents have been held prisoner in their offices, a conservative editor of a student newspaper has been beaten, the closed correspondence of university administrations has been exposed, and unpopular professors have had files searched and manuscripts destroyed. Presidents and deans who have taken the rebels to task have been called upon to resign, even though some of these administrators are themselves politically to the left of center.

Though the administration of Lyndon Baines Johnson probably did more for the American Negro than any since Abraham Lincoln's, the gulf between the black man and the American political system seemed to grow significantly wider while he was in office. During the summers of 1964, 1965, 1966 and 1967, America's major cities were plagued by violent riots in black ghettos. Similar troubles erupted after the slaying of the Reverend Martin Luther King, Jr. in the spring of 1968. On a different level, a good number of Negro leaders began during the Johnson era to reject white-Negro integration as a goal and took refuge in a demand for "black power."

The various antagonisms that we have been describing are still very much alive in the fourth year of the administration of Richard M. Nixon (except that there have been no large-scale Negro riots recently). Mr. Nixon is, of course, no left-winger; to the extent he openly espouses a political philosophy, it is that of "moderate conservatism." Yet, aside from his refusal to put a total end to American involvement in the Indochinese war and his emphasis on "getting tough" with suspected and potential criminals, he has not done much to antagonize persons who would describe themselves as protagonists of the welfare state. He is using Keynesian techniques and a wage-price freeze to try to end the country's stagflation and has seriously proposed the enactment of a guaranteed annual income bill and a comprehensive system of national health insurance. And most of President Johnson's War on Poverty program is still alive!

To confirm our thesis that a large number of persons in

the West who consider themselves left-wingers are hostile to the political system in which they live, we must turn to the European situation. First of all, despite the Conservative victory in the summer of 1970, the big country in which the left has most reason to be content is clearly Great Britain. The nation has a wide-ranging system of social services, including a scheme of almost-free medical care for all. Unemployment (especially when compared with the American situation) was low until 1971 and there is a fantastic quantity of public housing. Fuel, power, steel, and a large percentage of the transport industry is nationalized. Britain has to a good extent taken on the form of the socialist democracy ardently advocated for many years by Fabian socialists such as Beatrice and Sidney Webb. During almost the entire second half of the 60's, a Labor government was in power and was headed by a socialist intellectual, Mr. Harold Wilson.

However, much of even the British left is angry today. When Mr. Wilson attempted to give a speech at one of the major English universities he was bitterly heckled, not by Tories but by young men and women who were closer to Labor than to any other major British party. And college students have attempted to take the law into their own hands here, too. The *London Times* June 14, 1968, reports the following, for example:[2]

a. First year students at Nottingham College of Art and Design boycott an examination as a protest over the present system of art education.

b. Thre hundred students at Hull University end a five and one half day occupation of its administrative wing.

c. A group called the "Revolutionary Socialist Students Federation" is to hold its first meeting at the London School of Economics today.

d. The British National Union of Students informs university vice-chancellors and college principles that it will "apply sanctions" unless they start to discuss nine NUS demands before the end of the year.

Even in the France of the Fifth Republic there is much the average leftist could praise. The nation accepts the principle that the economy must be planned to assure full employment and industrial expansion and the airlines, railroads, and the Renault automobile company are state owned. In the field of foreign relations France has built bridges to Eastern Europe and it has condemned the U.S. adventure in Vietnam. Most important, General De Gaulle liquidated the Algerian war at the cost of antagonizing the army and many adherents of the far right. Thus it is not at all astonishing that some left wing Frenchmen can in all good faith sit in the National Assembly as members of the "Gaullist" party, the UNR.

But spring of 1968 brought gales which shook the Fifth Republic to its very roots. Once again the radical students were at the center of things. Several universities, including the Sorbonne in Paris, were seized by them, and Paris saw several weeks of street fighting between students and gendarmes. The violence spread to the right bank, and the Bourse was seized and a couple of police stations were besieged. The mood of rebellion infected the working class, many of the nation's largest factories were taken over by workmen, and a successful general strike brought about near chaos and forced the government to promise new elections and to bring troops in from Germany.

Belgium, Holland, West Germany and Sweden, all themselves prosperous welfare states, had similar stories to tell during the late 60's and early 70's, and there is no use repeating them in any detail. Now the obvious question is: What is the complaint which left-wing students, etc. have about regimes and institutions which are in the process of implementing reforms which have long been favorites of the left? An easy but superficial answer would be that the events we have been describing revolved about several discrete laments. Thus one could say that the student revolts in America and Great Britain were partly the result of the existence of Victorian rules regulating the students' conduct, partly the consequences of "examination fever," and partly (in America) a protest against conscription, the Vietnamese war, the Cambodian invasion and the massacre of four students at Kent State University in Ohio. And one could descend to an even more concrete level of analysis and point to Columbia University's construction of a gymnasium in New York City's Morningside Park (used mainly by Negroes) and its participation in a "cold war" organization called the Institute for Defense Analysis as the focal points of the unrest on that campus in spring, 1968. Likewise, the students at several other universities at which "sit-ins" occurred could be said to have acted as they did to force the administration to take more positive steps toward admitting Negroes.

As for the negro riots and the growing rejection of integration by Negro intellectuals, one can ascribe this to the all-too-slow disappearance of Negro poverty and white racism from the American scene. The French workers were simply demanding more pay, while their young confreres at the universities were protesting overcrowded conditions and sadly inadequate library facilities.

All these answers are true. But to stop with them would be unfortunate because to do so would miss the important point that those responsible for these acts of non-violent and not-so-non-violent civil disobedience all aver that those influenced by a set of policies should have a direct say in the determination of these policies and that this goal is undemocratically ignored by the institutions of today's liberal society. The French workers demand, in addition to more money, more representation on the governing boards of their respective firms. The French, British, and American students clamor for student representation on the faculty and administrative committees which frame the curriculum and which determine where the students must live, who can visit their rooms, and what they can smoke and drink. Typical is the set of demands made by the British Nation Union of Students. The

NUS calls for the following, among other things:

a. Effective student presence on all relevant college committees.

b. Student-staff control of discipline and joint discussion of course content and teaching methods.

c. Student control of their own organizations.

d. The abolition of outdated rules and regulations.

What is the American black power movement demanding? Some persons who are "black power" advocates want ultimate integration of the races while others favor the creation of a separate black state in the United States. Most renounce the use of violence except in self defense, but several do not. Yet they all seem to be agreed on one thing: the institutions that frame the rules that govern the Negro must be controlled by blacks themselves and will not be truly democratic until they are so controlled. The local grocery store determines what price the black will have to pay for the necessaries of life: very well, then, let's force the white owner to sell it to a black. The men at the local police station tell the ghetto children where they can and cannot congregate: okay, let's have only black policemen. Most importantly, the neighborhood school determines the future of the negro children. It must, therefore, be run by a group of black citizens from the neighborhood who will determine who is to teach them, what teaching methods shall be used, and what subjects are to be taught. Only if we control the schools in our areas, say the black power people, can we be certain that our children will not have to suffer the indignity of being taught by a white racist teacher, of having to read some irrelevant book about WASP Dick and Jane from the suburbs going to visit grandfather's farm, of being taught Greek but not African history, etc. This desire to set for himself the policy that controls his life is why the New York City Negro demanded that the schools in Brooklyn's Brownsville be run by a school board elected by the residents of Brownsville and not by the Board of Education of New York City — and is also the unexpressed reason why he has, on occasion, rioted. The black worker who is about to seize a television set from a flaming, white-owned store, the black professors and politicians who call for "black power," the American, British and French university students who occupy the administration building, the French worker who seizes his factory — all these are motivated, though they may not be aware of this similarity, by the wish to create a more democratic society in which they will draft for themselves the laws which grant them rights and impose duties upon them.

To put this in another way, a significant number of leftists in the Western world now rejects as undemocratic the slogan of the left during the first half of this century calling for abolishing poverty and exploitation by increasing the powers and extending the activities of the central government. (It is, of course, the means they have turned against, and not the end.) These persons we shall henceforth refer to interchangeably as "anti-bureaucratic radicals," "anti-bureaucratic left," "anti-statist radicals," "anti-statist left," "participatory democrats," and "decentralist socialists;" though those to whom these labels are applicable belong to diverse and uncoordinated groups or, in fact, may be isolated individuals who are members of no political association whatsoever. They are, perhaps, more frequently called the "New Left." However, this book will avoid this phrase because at present it produces in the mind of the average man images of dedicated revolutionaries making bombs to hurl at 10 Downing Street or the Pentagon, a mode of action which would shock many who hold the ideas we shall be considering in these pages.

The anti-bureaucratic radicals contend that the centralized welfare state and/or state socialism have been tried and proved wanting. Labor Britain, "Gaullist-Pompidouist" France, America's "Great Society" all suffer from the same basic flaw: they are centralized bureaucracies which are fundamentally undemocratic in the sense that the ordinary citizen has no voice in determining the policies that emanate from them — even though these may significantly affect his life. The freedom of speech and press, the representative assemblies, and the free elections which these nations feature may be good in some ways, but, in the eyes of the anti-bureaucratic left, they have not succeeded in transferring policy-making from the few to the many.

In place of the centralized social welfare state, these anti-bureaucratic radicals want to see, not capitalism, but what some of its members call a "participatory democracy." Only under a "participatory democracy" will the average man have a meaningful say in determining the laws that govern him and, therefore, only a "participatory democracy" is a true democracy. On the whole, these rebels against the old left would like to see functions now conducted for profit managed by the public, but would much prefer that it be an institution other than the national government which managed them. In fact, they are so hostile to the national government that in areas of larger nations which have a culture of their own many of them have joined a "separatist" movement. Though it would be absurd to say that a majority of those demanding regional autonomy or even independence in these provinces are left-wingers, radicals have been among those active in demanding freedom for Quebec[3] and Brittany.[4] There are so many men and women of the left in the Scottish Nationalist Party that its 1968 conference voted for a platform which stated that in an independent Scotland the national health service should be improved, the nationalized industries should remain nationalized, women should get the same pay as men and big landholdings should be broken up.[5] (The American sociologist, Nathan Glazer, is one of the several writers to note the essential ideological affinity between these demands for regional separatism and the student power, black power, etc., phenomena of the late sixties and early seventies.[6])

To continue, the anti-bureaucratic radicals, i.e., the radicals who deny that the central government should be the major agent of social change, demand that where an institution (e.g., school, welfare office) or an enterprise (e.g., a retail store) serves a neighborhood within the large political system, the neighborhood ought to control it. And where an institution is in a community but most of those who have contact with it come from outside the community (e.g., a factory or university), the institution should be controlled by those who work for it and/or by those who consume the goods and services it provides. It is the sum of the reforms mentioned in these two sentences that this book will analyze at length and henceforth refer to as "participatory democracy" or "decentralist socialism." (The reader will find a more detailed blueprint of this proposed social system in Chapter IV. We shall, incidentally, ignore the advantages and disadvantages of schemes such as "independent Scotland" or "autonomy for Brittany;" but we can note that some of the probable benefits and weaknesses of "participatory democracy" are immanent in these ideas, as well.) What the book will do first is describe certain thinkers of the last century and a half whose ideas are close to those put forth by today's participatory democrats. It will then define in detail one of the fundamental values of those who advocate "decentralist socialism" and, next, spend a good deal of time determining whether the implementation of this type of socialism would be likely to result in the widespread realization of that value, which we shall call a "self-governing citizenry." To aid us in this task, it will describe how several on-going attempts to put decentralist socialism into practice are faring. The look at these experiments shall enable us to discover what incidental benefits and evils it might produce. It will then explain why "participatory democracy" has become so popular with the left and, finally, weigh its pros and cons to see whether we should expend time and effort to transform it from an ideal into a reality.

The thought has no doubt been passing through the minds of many readers that it is unfair to link the ideal of participatory democracy to the radical, socialist left. After all, the liberal but hardly radical mayor of New York, John Lindsay, has recently made public a plan for the devolution of some political power from the city to the neighborhoods. Also some modern conservative thinkers such as the American Russell Kirk have urged their readers "to search for ways to turn the amorphous modern city into a series of neighborhoods, with common interests, amenities, and economic functions, . . . to bring back political coherence and decency to the city by decentralization" (and to) "stand for decentralization of industry" in order to achieve, among other things, "the humanizing of trade and manufacture, and the restoration of commuity."[7] This seems not too dissimilar from the 1962 "Port Huron Statement" of the Students for a Democratic Society (an organization much changed over the past decare), which asks "that the individual share in those social decisions determining the quality and direction of his life;" that political and economic life be based, among other things, on the principle "that politics has the function of bringing people out of isolation and into community, [and that] work . . . should be educative, not stultifying; creative, not mechanical; self-directed, not manipulated . . . "[8]

Nonetheless, there is a real justification for identifying "participatory democracy" (as we are defining that concept) with today's radical left. It involves not only a transfer of political power from broad to less encompassing political units but, among other things, a transfer of power over business enterprises from owners and managers to workers and consumers. And certainly Mr. Lindsay and Mr. Kirk would not be in favor of the last-mentioned switch. However, since the proposals of the anti-bureaucratic radicals on the one hand and of the above-mentioned moderates and conservatives on the other overlap, an analysis of a change effected by the one group that the other group would also favor is, at least to a limited extent, an analysis of the validity of the political theory of the other group. Therefore a study of neighborhood government in a country organized largely along the lines of decentralist socialism might be of some help in discovering whether neighborhood government would work in New York City even on the assumption that the United States economy remained controlled by private individuals and the central government. More to the point, research into the workings of neighborhood government in New York City, or into the workings of factories partially controlled by workers in a country in which the major economic decisions are made by the central government and private parties, may aid us in determining the feasibility of decentralist socialism considered as a whole. In fact, if we could carry out our plan of predicting whether decentralist socialism would be likely in practice to achieve certain ends only by looking to a nation in which it were fully accepted, we would have set for ourselves an impossible task, since there is at presnt no country in which that system is in operation on a full-fledged basis.

FOOTNOTES TO CHAPTER I

1. Press and Information Office of the Federal Government, *Facts About Germany*, 7th ed. (Bonn: Press and Information Service of the Federal Government, 1968), p. 235.

2. The *Times* (London), June 14, 1968, p. 8.

3. See Wilson, Frank L., "French-Canadian Separatism," *Western Political Quarterly*, 20:116-131, especially, p. 123, March 1967.

4. DeGaulle Plans Voter Reform, *New York Times*, Feb. 3, 1969, p. 1.

5. Bell, Colin, "Scots Nationalism and the Heather Roots," *New Statesman*, 75:754, June 7, 1968.

6. See article "For White and Black, Community Control is the the Issue," *New York Times Magazine*, April 27, 1969, p. 34ff.

7. *A Program for Conservatives* (Chicago: Henry Regney, 1962) pp. 162 and 218-19.

8. See Jacobs, Paul and Landau, Saul (eds.) — *The New Radicals* (New York: Random House Vintage Books, 1966) pp. 155-56.

II

PARTICIPATORY DEMOCRACY:
ITS INTELLECTUAL ANCESTRY

The call of the 1960's and 70's for the simultaneous abolition of the capitalist economy and of the powerful central
government is not a historical novelty. In fact, it was basic
in the thinking of many radicals during the nineteenth and
early twentieth centuries. This chapter will attempt to demonstrate this point; and will devote its second half to a
description of that school of thinkers that was perhaps the
most insistent and articulate in emphasizing the idea that
the good society is one where *both* production for private
profit *and* the centralized state are things of the past. We
are not contending here that today's anti-bureaucratic radicals have been guilty of "plagiarism"; or even that in some
mysterious way they have been subconsciously influenced by
the theorists we shall be talking about here. All we are trying to do is point out certain parallels between the ideas of
these current writers and the views of the men we are calling
their "precursors." An historical analysis such as this will be
of value to the historian of ideas who is faced with the necessity of classifying the numerous philosophies forming the
raw data with which he has to work. On a more practical
level, it could stimulate a few of today's anti-bureaucratic
leftists to examine the criticisms levied against their precursors, some of the particular reforms they suggested, and
the successes and failures of communities formed in accordance with their doctrines. And such an examination could

not help but make their own point of view clearer and more feasible.

Take first the British industrialist, social reformer, and trade union leader Robert Owen. Though he was emotionally a "paternalist" who felt that he knew much better than the working classes what type of life was good for them, his vision of the social arrangements that would be necessary for ending poverty involve anything but centralized state control of all the means of production. What was desirable to him, rather, was that the poor be resettled in small agricultural and manufacturing villages of between three hundred to two thousand souls, communities which were to be based upon the principles of "united labour, expenditure, and poverty, and equal privilege."[1] Though he hoped that the cost of establishing most of these villages would eventually be borne by the British government[2] and though he never expressed the desire to transform the British political system into one formally federal, these small socialist associations would not have been under the economic thumb of Westminster.

There are differences in life-style, temperament, and nationality betwen Owen and his fellow early-nineteenth-century social critic Charles Fourier, but the latter as much as the former eschews state socialism as a cure-all for the evils of this period. Fourier, like Owen, sees the small, cooperatively-owned agricultural and manufacturing village as the catalyst for his country's rejuvenation. These communities Fourier called "phalanxes," and were to be financed not by Paris but by the wealthier members of the phalanx themselves. They were to consist of between fifteen hundred to sixteen hundred individuals who would work at a variety of tasks during the day and whose remuneration would be labelled "dividends" rather than "wages."[3]

More overtly anti-statist than Owen and Fourier was the latter's countryman Pierre Proudhon. Some go so far as to term this forerunner of the anti-bureaucratic left of today an anarchist, and this point of view is not wholly without reason.

However, it would probably be more accurate to term him a socialist who wished to replace a centralized capitalist economy by locally-based producers cooperatives and the centralized state by a group of local governments. The central government is *per se* evil; but local politics are not necessarily tarred with the same brush. However, Proudhon did believe that his cooperatives should contract with one another when it was mutually advantageous to do so and that the local governments, too, should voluntarily work together for their common benefit.[4] Louis Blanc, a French socialist journalist, can also be numbered among the ideological ancestors of the modern "participatory democrats." To relieve unemployment among the poor, Blanc demanded that social workshops be set up which would provide the members of the proletariat with interesting and useful work. The State should set up and provide the initial financing for these producers cooperatives but it should have little to do with these institutions afterward. "After the first year, the associated laborers would freely choose administrators and leaders from among themselves; they would be occupied in discovering ways to expand the enterprise."[5] In other words, the control of industry after the demise of capitalism must be vested in the small groups who are most directly affected by the rules and regulations of the factories rather than in the bureaucrats in the nation's capital.

Current anti-bureaucratic radicalism could also be thought of as an intellectual descendant of nineteenth century anarchism. In the doctrines of Bakunin and Kropotkin, for example, one sees the same dislike not only of the capitalist system but also of centralized government that is so characteristic of organizations such as the Students for a Democratic Society. In the words of Bakunin " . . . The idea . . . of the State . . is the sacrifice of the natural liberty and interests of each component of individuals and of such comparatively small collective units as associations, communes and provinces — to the interests and freedom of everyone, to the prosperity of the great whole . . . But what actually be-comes of the whole at the moment when all individual and local interests have been sacrificed in order to compose it and coordinate themselves within it . . . It (becomes) the immolation of every individual, as of all local associations, the destructive abstraction of living society, the limitation, or rather, complete negation of life . . . "[6] And Kropotkin points out that in medieval times, when the most important political and economic units were the city, the village com-munity, and the artisan's guild, enormous advances were made in industry, commerce, and the arts. But then the centralized state came into being, destroying the sovereignty of village, city, and guild and placing them under the domi-nation of the corrupt representative of the king. "Under that fatal policy and the wars it engendered, whole regions, once populous and wealthy, were laid bare; rich cities be-come insignificant boroughs; . . . industry, art and knowl-edge fell into decay."[7] An idealization of the small group, and a loathing of the central government which threatens the autonomy and vitality of the small group, are views common to today's participatory democrats and to the anar-chists of a hundred years ago.

French syndicalism likewise bears a resemblance to the anti-bureaucratic left of the 1970's. Fernand Pelloutier, for example, placed his hopes in the "bourse du travail." A bourse was a local organization in which all the unions in one area were represented. Not only was it to act as an educa-tional and welfare association, but, moreover, it, and not the state, was to administer the industries in its region.[8]

Many people would juxtapose the "decentralist" or "com-munitarian" socialist theories we have been describing against that best known of socialist ideologies, Marxism. Yet Karl Marx did not pay much attention to the organization of the political and economic systems that would spring up in the wake of a socialist victory; and some of the things he did say when he bothered to concern himself with these matters indicate that he would have been content with a decentralized form of socialism. Thus Marx was extremely enthusiastic about the Paris commune of 1870, terming it "essentially a working class government, . . . the political form at last discovered under which to work out the economic emancipation of labor."[9] And what were the actions and proposals of the commune of which he approved? Included among these were the replacement of the old centralized state by a federation under which the central government would exercise a few functions and the local rural-urban areas ("communes") would exercise many. Also, the capitalist system of production was to be discarded in favor of a network of workers' cooperatives which would act together to insure the rational development of the nation's economy.[10] Likewise there are passages in the writings of Engels and even Lenin which indicate a dislike of the centralized socialist state. Thus the Russian quotes with approval the following propositions from Engel's comments on the Erfurt program of the German Social Democrats. " . . . From 1792 to 1798 each Department of France, each commune (*Gemeinde*), enjoyed complete self-government on the American model, and this is what we too must have. How self-government is to be organized and how we can manage without a bureaucracy has been shown to us by America and the First French Republic . . . "[11]

An orthodox Marxist socialist could theoretically embrace "participatory democracy," i.e., a politico-economic system where industry is controlled by the workers and where political policy is, on the whole, set by state, local and even neighborhood units of government. The Titoist Yugoslavs, for example, consider themselves *bona fide* Marxists and yet two decades ago they created "workers councils" in almost every Yugoslav factory and gave them the power to govern the concern. Why, then, do people instinctively feel that Marxism is a "centralist" creed?

Up to a point, the answer is a rather obvious one. The first, and probably the most important, of the *soi-disant*

"Marxist" nations is the U.S.S.R. Now the Soviet Union is in theory a federation of autonomous republics but functions in practice — more perhaps in Stalin's day than now — as a state which features a high degree of concentration of political power. There have at times been attempts to implement a decentralization of the economic system, but even the most radical of these endeavors has shunned the theory that the workers in a plant should manage it. And the general climate of terror and suppression that pervades the country is totally at odds with the libertarian, democratic assumptions of decentralist socialism.

But not only is "Marxism" associated in the popular mind with the political system that graces or disgraces Soviet Russia; there are also phrases in Marx and Engels themselves which seem to run counter to the decentralist ideas we have already quoted. There is, in the first place, Marx's assertion in the *Communist Manifesto* that immediately after the success of the proletarian revolution it will be desirable to institute the following. " . . . 5. Centralization of credit in the hands of the *State*. . . . 6. Centralization of the means of communication and transport in the hands of the *State*. . . . 7. Extension of factories and instruments of production owned by the *State*. . . . "[12] (Emphasis mine.) There is in the same document a reference to Fourier and Owen as "utopians," still dreaming "of founding isolated 'phalansteres,' establishing 'home colonies' . . . pocket editions of the New Jerusalem."[13] (It is probable, however, that what Marx was attacking in these men was not their love for the small community but their inability to appreciate the significance of the phenomenon of class antagonism.) And, finally, there is Engel's claim in *Socialism*: *Utopian and Scientific* that by virtue of its revolution "the proletariat seizes political power and turns the means of production into state property."[14] Thus those who believe in socialism "administered from above" can defend themselves by pointing to passages from the founders of "scientific socialism;" but it is important to realize that the same is true for those who are attracted to a socialism where policy is "set from below."[15]

Ironically, the group of political philosophers whose views may be closest to those of many modern anti-bureacratic radicals is apparently ignored in their writings and speeches (except for those of that "old" anti-bureaucratic radical Paul Goodman). I refer to the school of Guild Socialists which flourished in England between 1905 and 1922 but which now gets at most a couple of paragraphs in the average textbook on the history of political thought. And the first individual to make a thorough-going attempt to formulate a Guild Socialism that was applicable to the twentieth century was the engineer, S. G. Hobson, who did so in articles which appeared in the *New Age* magazine beeginning in 1912 and were converted into a book entitled *National Guilds*.

Hobson's solution to the problem of how to eradicate capitalism without relying upon an overgrown and thus freedom-threatening superstate was essentially very simple: each industry should be placed under the control of a democratically organized guild (i.e., trade union) embracing the industry. In other words, it was his belief that everyone associated with an industry should be a member of a decentralized guild having the authority to manage that particular industry, and, moreover, that the guilds and *not* the state, should maintain their members in sickness, idleness, and old age.[16] The role of the socialist state is merely to own the land, buildings, and machinery utilized by the various guilds, to provide cultural amenities and higher education for its citizens, to enact civil and criminal legislation, and to have control over the army and navy and questions of foreign affairs. (All of the state's activities are to be financed by a tax levied on the guilds as payment for their use of its property.[17]) Disputes between guilds will be settled by a Guild Congress representative of all the guilds:[18] where a guild violated public policy — e.g., by refusing to supply a particular commodity or by arbitrarily shipping this commodity to one

locality rather than to another — the state may employ force
or the threat thereof to remedy the situation.[19]

Beside Hobson, the other significant theorist of Guild Socialism was G. D. H. Cole. Cole's first detailed version of
Guild Socialism appeared in the *New Age* between 1914 and
1917, in articles which formed the basis of his book entitled
Self Government in Industry. His answer to the question of
how to put an end to the evils of the capitalist system without at the same time excessively increasing the powers of the
state is quite similar, in essence, to Hobson's. That is, the
control of each industry should be left to a democratically
organized decentralized guild, while the state should merely
own the property that the guilds will use. And the guild,
rather than the state, should insure that its members are
provided for when sick, old, and when work is slack.[20] So far,
there is no real disagreement with Hobson: the disciple has
up to this point followed the master.

Where *Self-Government in Industry* departs to a large extent from the doctrines of Hobson is in its conception of the
state's proper role vis-a-vis the economy. Hobson considers
Parliament the sovereign organ of the community. Although,
as a general rule, it is to practice extreme laissez faire with
respect to economic matters and leave questions of production to the guilds, *it,* and not, for example, the Guild Congress, has the ultimate authority to prevent guilds, individuals, and other groups from affecting the economy in a way
that runs counter to public policy.[21]

However, the function of Cole's state is solely to represent
man as consumer. It thus obviously must be given some say
in determining prices and the flow of investment. But the
Guild Congress, the representative of man as producer, must
likewise be handed some authority with respect to these matters, for he who fabricates an item certainly has an interest
in these questions, and one which is different from the consumer's and which the latter's agent accordingly cannot adequately represent. Therefore, Cole argues, the ultimate sov-

ereignty *vis-a-vis* these problems — and, in fact, as regards all economic matters — must reside in a Joint Congress equally representative of the state and of the Guild Congress.[22]

A bit later in his Guild Socialist career, Cole, on a verbal level at least, turned even more against the state and to a position which reminds one of today's anti-bureaucratic left. This position is that most political and economic power is to be vested in numerous small-scale, local organizations that represent producers and/or consumers. The four "consumers" organizations are the Cooperative Societies, public utility councils, Cultural Councils, and health councils. The workers, of course, will be grouped into democratically organized, self-governing guilds, with branches in each factory and in each locality. He adds, however, that when consumers' association and producers' organization disagree on a question, they are to enter into negotiations to solve this dispute. For example, if the Chicago area dairy producers guild and Chicago consumers cooperative were at odds on the question of how much the latter should pay the former for its milk or of whether the former should concentrate on cheddar rather than muenster cheese they should sit down together and talk. Only if they could not settle the matter this way would the quarrel be referred to the body which has the ultimate power to make authoritative decisions on political and economic questions — an organization which Cole calls the commune. This commune, except for the fact that its members are to represent producers and consumers organizations, is, frankly, very much like the polity of today in power and function, and is to function on the national, regional and local levels. However, he seems to think that the mere fact it is called "commune" rather than "state" will mean that more decisions will be made by the local consumers and producers groups; and in any case he does assert that the local and regional communes will be much busier than the national body.[23] For these reasons, despite the introduction of the national commune, *Guild Socialism Restated* remains a work whose basic philosophy is close to that of "participatory democracy."

In 1929 Cole declared that he was an "ordinary" socialist rather than a Guild Socialist — i.e., he came to admit that socialism brought into being by the parliamentary state was the most practicable way of solving the pressing problems of Great Britain and the world. However, he retained in his new ideology some of the major tenets of the decentralist, Guild Socialist faith. Most importantly, he favored workers control of industry, which to him involved a system under which the workers in each factory would elect their foremen and would choose a works council to take care of plant discipline and the welfare services in the enterprise. In addition, each work group was to allocate its tasks among its members and to receive a lump sum from the employer which the members would share out among themselves.[24] He also called for the division of the large city into neighborhood units which would have power to maintain community centers, civic restaurants, health centers, day nurseries, and local streets.[25] In fact, as he noted at the end of his life, he always remained a Guild Socialist at heart, believing that a totally decentralized political and economic system was the best one imaginable but that for practical purposes all that we could hope for in the near future was a socialism which contained centrifugal as well as centripetal elements.[26] And there is no doubt that his lifelong hatred of the capitalist system, his suspicion of the centralized, bureaucratic state, his belief in the importance of workers' management of industry and in decentralization of political power and his advocacy of "neighborhood" autonomy all make him an ideological elder cousin to the anti-bureaucratic left of today. There are, of course, some differences between Cole and the "participatory democrats," but we shall omit any mention of these until our discussion of the possible adverse side-effects of the implementation of their ideal social system.

To sum up, we have seen that the political thought of the

anti-bureaucratic radicals of the second half of the twentieth century is far from the first to repudiate both the profit motive and rigid control of the economy by the national government. In a sense, it is an addition to a well-established town rather than a pioneer village.[27] To say this, however, is in no sense to prejudge the quality of the efforts of these radicals of the current era. The worth of a political theory does not necessarily depend upon its providing us with a completely new way of viewing social or political life: it will contain merit even if it does no more than give us with sensible solutions to some pressing dilemmas. The question of whether the ideas of the anti-bureaucratic radicals furnish such solutions cannot, of course, be answered until we have analyzed these in much more depth than we have up to this point.

FOOTNOTES TO CHAPTER II

1. Owen, Robert, *A New View of Society and Other Writings* (London: J. M. Dent & Sons, 1927) pp. 264-267.

2. *Ibid.,* p. 166.

3. See the selection from Fourier's writings in Fried, Albert and Sanders, Ronald (eds.) *Socialist Thought* (New York: Anchor Books, 1964) pp. 142-151.

4. See Philip Taft's discussion of Proudhon's political and economic philosophy, pp. 103-109 of *Movements for Economic Reform* (New York: Rinehart & Co., 1950).

5. See the introduction to his *Organization of Labor,* 1848 *edition,* pp. 232-233 of Fried and Sanders (ed.), *op. cit.*

6. See the letter of his excerpted at pp. 341-344 of Fried and Sanders (ed.) *op. cit.*

7. See his *Mutual Aid,* pp. 349-50 of Fried and Sanders (ed.) *op. cit.*

8. See Taft, *op. cit.,* p. 177.

9. See his *Civil War in France,* p. 369 of Lewis Fever (ed.) : *Marx and Engels* (New York: Doubleday, 1959).

10. *Ibid.,* pp. 366-370.

11. See Lenin's *State and Revolution,* pp. 158-59 of Mendel,

Arthur P. (ed.) *Essential Works of Marxism* (New York: Bantam Books, 1961).

12. Mendel, *loc cit.,* p. 32-33.
13. *Ibid.,* p. 42.
14. *Ibid.,* p. 77.
15. Many of the present-day advocates of "participatory democracy" are fond of quoting from the writings of the pre-Communist Manifesto Marx about one's "alienation" from what he produces, in his work, and from his fellow man and of asserting that participatory democracy is necessary to cure these forms of estrangement.
16. According to both Hobson and G. D. H. Cole, the professions, the non-factory trades, and the distributive trades are also to be organized into guilds.
17. What has appeared so far in this paragraph is based upon S. G. Hobson, *National Guilds* (2nd ed., London: G. Bell & Sons, 1917), pp. 132-37, p. 150, pp. 256-58.
18. *Ibid.,* pp. 231-32.
19. S. G. Hobson, An Interlude with Mr. Cole, *New Age,* 22:286, Feb. 7, 1918.
20. G. D. H. Cole, *Self Government in Industry,* p. 90.
21. See e.g. S. G. Hobson, Nation, State, and Government, *New Age,* 23:5, May 2, 1918.
22. G. D. H. Cole, *Self Government in Industry,* 5th rev. ed., pp. 116-17, 135-36, p. 240.
23. *Guild Socialism Restated* (London: Leonard Parsons, 1921), p. 136, pp. 141-42, p. 148.
24. See his *National Coal Board* (London: Gollancz n.d.) p. 56; *Case for Industrial Partnership,* (London: Macmillan, 1957) pp. 37-50; Workers' Control and Self Government in Industry, pp. 15-17 (London: Gollancz, 1933).
26. See his *History of Socialist Thought,* Vol. IV, Part I, p. 10.
27. An honorary resident of this town was Thomas Jefferson. Though no socialist, he was, of course, a member of the "left" of his day and penned the following passage — a precursor of the American decentralist socialists: "Divide the countries into wards of such size as that every citizen can attend, when called on, and act in person. Ascribe to them the government

of their wards in all things relating to themselves exclusively. A justice, chosen by themselves, in each, a constable, a military company, a patrol, a school, the care of their own poor, their own portion of the public roads, the choice of one or more jurors to serve in some court. . . . will relieve the county administration of nearly all its business, will have it better done, and by making every citizen an acting member of the government, and in the offices nearest and most interesting to him, will attach him by his strongest feelings to the independence of his country, and its republican constitution." From a letter to Samuel Kercheval, written July 12, 1916, and appearing at p. 369, 371-2 of Mason, Alpheus (ed.) *Free Government in the Making*, 1st ed. (New York: Oxford University Press, 1949).

III

THE SELF-GOVERNING CITIZEN

We must first go more deeply into the question of what the fundamental values of the participatory democrats of today are. Every political theorist views certain goals as basic and asserts that the society he wants will be conducive to the realization of these and that the societies he criticizes will in one way or another thwart their achievement. Thomas Hobbes, for example, maintained that physical security was essential and that without a strong centralized state physical security could not be guaranted. What goals do the anti-bureaucratic radicals visualize as fundamental? Not all of them have made their response to their query explicit. However, in the tracts of groups such as the American Students for a Democratic Society one can discover the answer. (We noted earlier that the SDS has much changed since 1961. When in this book we speak of this organization we do not refer to the Maoist Progressive Laborites or to the Weathermen or other factions into which it has split now but to the SDS of 1961 to 1964 or so. It is not that the Progressive Laborite or the Weathermen necessarily reject participatory democracy; it is just that the "original" SDS members devoted more time and energy to making clear what this ideal connotes and thus it is their efforts which are more important for the purpose of this particular volume.)

To the Students for a Democratic Society, man is *not* a "thing to be manipulated," although in the modern world "men have been completely manipulated into incompetence."[1]

Under both American welfare capitalism and British state socialism, to say nothing of Russian communism, men are mere puppets. What is neded, therefore, as we saw in Chapter I, is a social system that will make them autonomous by giving them the power to shape the policy decisions that concern their lives. Moreover, "human relationships should involve fraternity and honesty," but "loneliness, estrangement, isolation describe the vast distance between men today."[2] Therefore the new social system must be one that will encourage the average man to work with others and thus be rescued from loneliness and alienation. And, hopefully, participatory democracy, with its active neighborhood governments, its workers' control of industry, and its student-faculty control over education will be just the method to achieve these two fundamental goals of promotion of community and the development of individuals who frame the laws to which they are subject.[3]

Incidentally, the Guild Socialist G. D. H. Cole favored decentralization of the socialist state of the future because it was a technique for insuring the realization of these basic values of fraternity and of what we shall henceforth often refer to as a "self-governing citizenry"—i.e., a situation where each man *as an individual* shapes the rules and regulations that are of concern to him. For example, he criticized parliamentary democracy on the ground that " . . . It has largely failed: it is the very fact that it has not made effective the will of the individual citizen that has caused the opposition to it to die down."[4] Late in his life he asserted that "In social philosophy I have always been a pluralist . . . insisting that the proper basis of a free society must be functional, with power and responsibility split up . . . so as to leave the individual free to choose his own primary allegiance instead of being subjected more than is unavoidable to a centralized authority over which he is too weak to have any effective control."[5] In an article originally written during World War II he contended that " . . . real democracies have either to be small, or to be broken up into small, human groups in which men and women can know and love one another. If human societies get too big, and are not broken up in that way, the human spirit goes out of them . . . "[6])

But to return to our main theme, let us repeat that the participatory democrats of today are firmly attached to two ideals we can call respectively "community" and a "self-governing citizenry." We shall not be concerned with "community" until our concluding chapter. It is surely an important ideal, but, because of the absence of pertinent data, we are able to say very little beyond what will appear there about whether it is likely to be positively correlated with participatory democracy. What we *shall* be involved with is the connection between participatory democracy and the first-mentioned goal, the growth of a "self-governing citizenry." First of all, who can be considered a "self-governing citizen," that is, one who *as an individual* helps mold the politics governing his life? Before a more precise definition is given, we must explain why we emphasize the words "as an individual." It is clear that in most non-totalitarian societies, organized groups of individuals do have political and economic power. It may be valid, for example, to contend with C. Wright Mills that major foreign and military policy decisions in the United States are made by a small, overlapping elite of military men, businessmen, and politicians; but in the domestic sphere, at least, organized interest groups either call the tune or, at the very least, play first violin in the orchestra. It is impossible to think of one major piece of legislation passed by the United States government whose shape was not affected by the interaction of several pressure groups either supporting or opposing the measure. Groups such as the labor unions and the Conference of Mayors pushed a bill through in 1966 to creat a cabinet-level Department of Transportation; but the railroads, the shipping lines, the airlines, the Army Corps of Engineers flexed their muscles to insure that the Secretary of Transportation had no power over the several transportation industries.[7] Likewise, consumers groups obtained during the same year the enactment of a Motor Vehicle Safety Bill, but the American Motor Vehicle Manufacturers Association saw to it that the act contained no criminal penalties for its violation. And group conflict prevails even within the military-industrial complex: Company X wages bitter war in the halls of the Pentagon and the Congress with Company Y over the question of who should develop a supersonic airliner or anti-missile defense system.

But though the AFL-CIO, the Conference of Mayors, the railroads, the airlines, Boeing Corporation of Seattle, etc. may have had something to do with framing the acts described above, most of us taken as individuals did not. We may be union members and hold stock in a railroad, an airline, and/or the Boeing Corporation, but our voices, if indeed they were even raised, were not heard in the debate over these bills. The point that the power of a group does not prove the possession of power by most of the group's members taken individually, of course, is obvious; but it needs reiterating because the individual who is worried by a feeling of powerlessness is often told that he is strong because, e.g., his union is vigorous or because he can help elect the board of directors and attend the shareholders meetings of the company in which he holds stock.

Turning now to a more precise definition of the self-governing citizen, a definition limited, for simplicity's sake, to the political sphere, we have to distinguish between two situations. As is well-known, a direct democracy is one where the body that is legally responsible for the framing of policy for a group or community is the entire group of adults making up that group or community. To an American, the old-time New England town meeting, where all the adult citizens of the town met at least once a year to make the laws for that political entity, is the classic example. Where an institution or community is governed according to the principles of direct democracy, it is reasonable in many cases to call a citizen politically self-governing, i.e., helping as an individual to frame political policy, where he regularly attends the legislative sessions and on occasion expresses his point of view on a political issue or issues.

However, most institutions or polities are not organized according to the principles of direct democracy, which is in practice very difficult to implement when there are more than a couple of hundred people involved. Much more common, at least in countries which reject the notions of dictatorship or democracy, is the practice of representative ("republican") democracy, where laws are made by freely-elected representatives of the people meeting at certain intervals in accordance with certain rules, procedures and constraints. It is, therefore, of more practical importance as well as of greater theoretical interest and difficulty, to determine when one who is a member of an organization or community organized according to the principle of representative democracy can be viewed as a self-governing citizen. It makes sense to call him or her politically self-governing, i.e., helping as an individual to frame political policy, when his or her views on one or more issues that can reasonably be called "political" are among the reasons why at least one member or one employee of the governments with jurisdiction over him votes or decides in the way specified by these views. To make this rather tangled and abstract idea clearer, we must first explain a couple of the words it contains. The words we shall clarify also appear in the definition of the individual who is self governing in a direct democracy; and consequently the following explanation will apply to that definition, too. However, unless the contrary is clear from the context, a mention of the definition of the self-governing citizen shall henceforth be a mention of the definition of the self-governing citizen in a representative democracy.

The definition of the self-governing citizen: explanation of terms

If the reader will once again glance at the last paragraph, he will see that the definition of "self-governing citizen" it sets forth employs the word "issues." Now what is an "issue" for purpose of this definition? It is necessary to ask this question because political, economic, etc., policy can be subdivided into thousands of issues, some of which are relatively general and can themselves be broken down into sub-issues and sub-sub issues. Take, for example, the case of an institution whose affairs seem simple, a company that manufactures nuts, bolts, nails, screws, hammers, planes and similar items that are used by carpenters and home repairmen. The policy that emanates from this corporation is really made up of numerous issues and sub-issues: e.g., should we sell in this area of the country rather than that; should we increase our production of screws and reduce our production of nails; if we do increase our production of screws, what sizes should we concentrate upon; should we purchase the assets of a bankrupt rival; should we diversify our product line; should we improve working conditions in our factories. (The latter can be analyzed into sub-problems of whether we should give the workers longer coffee breaks, improve toilet and cafeteria facilities, set up a company recreation room, etc.)

If so many issues face the officers of a small manufacturing concern, imagine how many more confront, for example, the legislature of the State of New York, the Congress of the United States or the British Parliament. A major bill passed by Congress is really an attempt to meet hundreds of issues. For example, take the Fair Housing bill enacted into law in 1968. This act, on a superficial level, tackled one major question: ought the government of the United States make it illegal for private persons to discriminate on racial or religious grounds in the sale of real estate? But the legislators had to consider many narrower questions in the course of enacting it: what types (all homes, only multi-unit dwellings, only new homes, etc.) of real estate should be covered by the act? Should discrimination be prohibited on religious as well as racial grounds? What agency should be primarily responsible for the enforcement of the law? How much should be appropriated for the enforcement of the law? When should it come into effect? What sanctions should exist for its violation? Even more complicated, of course, are laws which set up programs such as a National Health Service or which aid elementary and secondary education.

For the purpose of our definition of modern anti-bureaucratic radicalism's ideal of the self-governing citizen, an "issue" is any question, no matter how narrow, that an institution or community is asked to solve. This term "issue" includes major questions as well as much more limited ones that are included in the broader question. For example, whether the government ought to provide free medical care to its citizens is an issue; whether this free medical care should be financed by general taxation or by contributions to a special fund is an issue; whether the doctors who participate in the scheme should be considered national, state, or local employees is an issue; and whether a clinic at which such free care is provided should be erected at 49th Street and 10th Avenue or at 50th Street and 11th Avenue is also an issue.

It will be remembered that our definition also is limited to a statement of when an individual is "politically" self-governing, and that to be politically self governing he or she must have a voice on issues that can be "political." Without attempting to elucidate this amorphous word, we can make the obvious point that there are economic, religious, social, as well as political institutions in every society and that one with power over an economic institution may have little power over a political unit. Thus our hypothetical nuts-and-bolts manufacturer may have a good deal to say about how his firm is run but little control over his city government. Our definition confines itself to a definition of political self-government for reasons of style alone. Neither the author nor the anti-bureaucratic radicals who call for the development of a self-governing citizenry think that only the political sphere of life is of consequence and, as we shall soon see, they favor shaping social institutions so as to make the individual sovereign in other spheres, too. Actually, couching our definition of the self-governing citizen in terms of the political does not mean that we will be unable to test whether an institution designed, for example, to allow workers and students to frame some of the rules and regulations that apply to them at the business, factory, or school, is successful in this regard. This definition can easily be converted so as to become applicable to these areas of life outside the sphere of the political. For example, an individual self-governing at work (or, active as an individual in framing the rules that govern him at work) is one whose views on one or more issues that concern life in the enterprise are among the reasons why at least one individual on the body (e.g., factory works council) with power to resolve these issues votes or decides in the way specified by these views. And an individual self-governings as a consumer of goods and services is one whose views on one or more issues that concern the goods or services he receives or would like to receive are among the reasons why at last one individual on the body (e.g., elective board of directors of a consumers co-op) with power to resolve these issues votes or decides on the way specified by these views. Finally, an individual can be termed self-governing generally when his policy views are among the reasons why at least one individual on each, or at least on a significant proportion, of the institutions which frame the rules that affect his life votes or decides in the way specified by these views.

Politically self-governing citizens under our definition

To reiterate, the modern anti-bureaucratic left's ideal of a politically self-governing citizen is being defined by us for a representative democracy as a man or woman whose views on one or more issues that can reasonably be called political are among the reasons why at least one member or one employee of the governments with jurisdiction over him votes or decides in the way specified by these views. Construing a couple of terms in this definition, such as we have just finished doing, is helpful but not sufficient. To make it more comprehensible, we must now note several particular situations and then apply it to these situations to determine whether the relevant individuals are or are not politically self-governing.

A. Assume that Green is a member of the New York City Council. As this is a legislative body which has some real independence. Green is a self-governing citizen. No matter how much he believes that he should adhere to the wishes of the voters, every member of a representative legislature which has some independence falls into this category of self-governing citizen, since his own attitudes or interests are almost bound to be among the reasons why on at least one issue he votes in a certain way. Surely, for example, one reason why midwestern Republicans in the American Senate and House tend to vote against measures such as national health insurance is that they personally believe that it is not the duty of government to provide its citizens with cheap medical care.

Now, turning from the legislator to his constituents, our definition leads to the following results:

B. Let us assume that Jones is the editor of the local newspaper. He is opposed to having the planned new expressway built through the city's major park and phones one of the members of the city council to inform him of this. The city councillor, who had planned to vote for the park route, casts his ballot against it as a result of this phone call. Jones, the editor, can be said to be politically self-governing even though the reason for his success was not the inherent persuasiveness of his arguments or his sparkling personality but the councillor's perception of him as an individual with the ability to advance or destroy the councillor's political career. Of course, we would reach the same result had Jones been listened to because he was a union leader or the leader of the local chamber of commerce.

C. Keeping with the same basic facts as in "B", let us assume that the phone call from Jones is not in itself sufficient to change the councillor's mind. But Williams, a prominent Protestant minister, and Father O'Keefe, the priest in the largest Catholic church in the city, drop in on him and make it clear that they, too, dislike the proposed route. In the face of the position taken by the press magnate and the two influential clerics, the councillor abandons his initial stance. Jones, Williams, and O'Keefe all can be said to be politically self-governing, for each man's view on the expressway controversy is among the "reasons" for the politician's change of heart. (To put this idea a little more generally, an individual can be said to be politically self-governing even though his statement of views on an issue was only a necessary rather than a sufficient condition of a legislator's voting in a way consistent with these views.) However, if our councillor had changed his mind because of the large number of letters he had received on the matter and would have voted against the route even if Jones, Williams, and O'Keefe had never contacted him, these three gentlemen could not be said to be politically self?governing as a consequence of these communications. Moreover, no one of the individuals who wrote these letters can be said to have become self-governing. It is not really *his* letter which convinced the councilman, but the letters *en masse*.

D. Let us suppose that the councilman had changed his mind because he knew Jones, the editor, was antagonistic to the original routing even though the latter had never made his views public in any way. Under our definition Jones would be a politically self-governing citizen. However, suppose he had misread Jones' position and changed his mind under the *mistaken* impression that Jones was against the original route. Jones could not be said to be politically self-governing as a result of this incident because it was not *his* views which caused the switch. However, one could assume from the fact that the councilman was very worried about Jones' position that Jones has probably won him over on other occasions which, of course, *would* make him politically self-governing.

E. Let us suppose that Smith is a member of the local NAACP and that he convinces the governing board of that Association to oppose a pay raise for policemen. As a result of the Association's antagonism to the bill authorizing such a raise, Wilson, a city councillor, votes against it. It is reasonable to consider Smith a politically self-governing citizen because it is reasonable to say that his view on the question of higher wages for policemen was "among the causes" of Wilson's "nay." More generally, a member of an organization is politically self-governing when he plays an important role in persuading a group or individual to take a position which it (he) later persuades a legislator to adopt.

F. Using the facts set forth in "B," assume that the city council as a whole approved the original route, though the member whom Jones contacted voted no, and that the measures favored by the newspaper usually are rejected by the council and *vice versa*. Jones, under our definition, would be politically self-governing even though his political power would admittedly be slight. In general, he who can sway a legislator to his side will be politically self-governing under our definition even though that legislator is usually on the minority in the legislature itself.

G. Let us assume that Mazza persuades his councilman to vote for a clause in a education appropriation act providing that $500 of the appropriated funds shall be used to repair the baseball field of Babe Ruth High School and that his conversation with his representative did not touch upon any other item in the statute. Under our definition, Mazza would be politically self-governing since his views on an issue arguably political are among the reasons why the councilman voted that way on the issue. More generally, under our definition an individual is politically self-governing even though his success with a legislator relates to part of a bill only.

H. Let us assume that Mazza in "G" supra acts as he does

simply because he likes teenagers to have a place to play baseball and that neither he nor any member of his family is
likely ever to use the high school's diamond. He is still politically self-governing, simply because he convinced his representative to vote in a certain way on an issue which interested him. There is nothing in our definition that asserts that
one cannot have a view on an issue, within the meaning of
the definition, unless the resolution of the issue will foster
or impede his material interests or his way of living.

I. Let us assume that the councilman whom Mazza speaks
to favored the repair of the field anyway. Mazza is politically
self-governing if the councilman might have changed his
mind had he not talked to him. More generally whether an
individual, X, who urges his legislator to vote for (against)
a bill the latter favored (opposed) anyway is politically self-
governing depends on whether the lawmaker might have altered his views had he not talked to X. If the chances are
at least fair that he would have altered his position but for
X's prodding, X can be said to be politically self-governing.

J. Let us assume that Mazza could have convinced his
councilman to vote the appropriation for the repair of the
diamond if he had contacted him but that he did not bother
doing so. We cannot say that Mazza is politically self-governing simply because he could have had his way if he had
troubled to exert himself. There is a difference between being potentially politically self-governing and being actually
so. The individual must exert himself to transform possibility
into actuality: he must speak or write to his legislator or run
for public office himself. The only person who sits back who
still can be called politically self-governing is he about whose
position the politician worries even though it has not been
made public, e.g., the head of the town's largest factory or
the minister of its largest church. And it is a sure thing that
even these men have attempted to be politically influential
in the past — for if they had always been unconcerned about
public affairs the powers-that-be would not worry about their
reaction now.

K. Let us assume that Swenson is of a middle-class home-
owner in a small American town. This gentleman may wholeheartedly approve of his council's rejection of every proposal
that might lead to a rise in the property tax, and moreover,
the parallelism between his attitudes and those of the council
may well make him feel that the city's government is not
something "alien" to him. But we need more information
before we can say that he is "politically self-governing," for
we cannot say offhand that he personally or he working in
conjunction with a couple of others made any councillor
"anti-tax."

L. Let us assume that the Swenson of "K," supra, is a member of his town's Chamber of Commerce, that both he and
the Chamber are ardently opposed to a proposal to grant a
subsidy to the ailing local public transportation company,
and that the Chamber does convince the council to reject
this idea. We still cannot say without more ado that Swenson
is politically self-governing. (If he played an important role
in persuading the Chamber that the subsidy was pernicious,
then he would, of course, fall into this category.)

We have so far limited our analysis of who is and who is
not politically self-governing to a study of the legislature and
its constituents. But in the modern world many decisions
made by "the government" are made by the executive branch
and even by the courts. It was not the Congress of the United
States but President Johnson who committed the United
States to intervene in Vietnam in a massive scale and it was
not Congress but the United States Supreme Court which initially held that racially segregated public schools inherently
deprive children of the minority race of the equal protection
of the laws. On a less dramatic level, it is the Federal Communications Commission and not Congress which really decides which of two competing applicants shall be licensed to
broadcast over a particular TV channel and it is a federal
court and not Congress that determines whether the Commission's award of the license is reasonable or arbitrary. All

this is why our definition of the politically self-governing citizen uses the phrase "at least one member of the *governments* with jurisdiction over him" instead of "at least one member of the *legislatures* with jurisdiction over him." To do otherwise would be to be guilty of denying the status of politically self-governing citizen to the man who convinces the President of the United States to sign a bill authorizing the expenditure of billions of dollars on four-lane expressways but granting it to the person who gets a city councilman to vote in favor of a measure requiring all the city's street signs to be of a certain size!

In general, we can say that all judges, and all members of the executive branch of a government who have some policy-making prerogatives, are politically self-governing. A member of the executive branch is a policy maker when he, for example, jointly or in conjunction with others frames rules which are applicable to more than one instance or when he in practice has the final decision as to whether or not an individual should be subject to a penalty or afforded a benefit and that decision has implications for other cases. (This list is not exhaustive.) Thus the members of the Interstate Commerce Commission are policy-makers and consequently self-governing citizens: they determine safety standards for railroads and act upon requests for increases and discontinuances in service. The same can be said about the Federal Aviation Administrator, who approves safety regulations for aircraft. On the other hand, the postman who delivers the mail to your door before noon every morning is clearly not a policy maker *qua* postman; and thus we cannot say that without more information about him that he is policitically self-governing. We are not contending here, of course, that it is always clear whether a particular public employee or official is a "policy maker;" and there are obviously many, many borderline cases, e.g., the postmaster of a medium-sized town. All that we are saying is that when an employee of an executive branch of a government is a policy maker, he is (with one exception which will be noted in a few pages) a politically self-governing citizen. We assume, I think rightly, that some of his decisions will be at least in part the product of his own views and interests.

Turning now to the question of when the citizen who comes into contact with a bureaucrat can by virtue of that relationship be said to be a politically self-governing citizen, we find that under the definition with which we are working the situations in which an affirmative answer can be given are analogous to those which were discovered in the citizen-legislator relationship. If, for example, the New York State Highway Commission has the authority to determine the routes of new highways, and Editor Jones convinces a Commissioner to vote in favor of building a road through a slum rather than through a park, Jones is a self-governing citizen even though the Commissioner was swayed by his view of Jones' power rather than by the eloquence of his rhetoric. And even if it takes the combined oratory of Editor Jones, Pastor Williams, and Father O'Keefe to push the Commissioner, each of these "guardians of the public interest" can be said to be politically self-governing.

Likewise, if the Vice-President in charge of engineering of an auto manufacturing concern convinces the American Automobile Manufacturers Association that it ought to protest to the United States Secretary of Transportation about one of his proposed auto safety regulations, and as a result of its protest the Secretary decides to revoke the proposed regulation, that Vice-President in charge of engineering can be said to be a self-governing citizen. But once again the mere fact that one is in sympathy with a particular decision or the general tenor of the decisions issued by an administrative agency does not make him self-governing. Our middle-class home-owner may be overjoyed by the state welfare department's adoption of strict criteria of eligibility for welfare but his delight at this turn of affairs does not automatically turn him into a self-governing citizen.

However, a couple of remarks must be made about the citizen who can be said to be self-governing as a result of his dealings with the bureaucracy that were not appropriate for our discussion of the citizen-legislator relationship. In perhaps nine out of ten cases, the individual who requests that a civil servant do something for him will find his petition automatically granted, usually because the rules and regulations that the governmental employee is supposed to obey make it clear that the individual has the right to what he asks for. In this case, the affirmative action taken by the bureaucrat does not make the citizen politically "self-governing;" implicit in our definition of that phrase is the idea of sometime antagonism or at least scepticism on the part of the ultimately compliant governmental official toward the view of the citizen. Thus when a man aged sixty-five goes into a social security office and asks that he start receiving old-age insurance benefits and, after a check of his records, monthly checks begin flowing to him without any additional exertion on his part, he cannot be said to have become politically "self-governing:" politics implies conflict or true potential of conflict and this is true whether politics involves orders from a totalitarian state to its citizens or a command by a citizen that is obeyed by one of his rulers. On the other hand, if our gentleman of sixty-five is denied his pension under an administrative regulation but later obtains it by convincing a higher-level bureaucrat that the initial decision-maker misunderstood the regulation, then he would be politically self-governing. To sum up, one does not become politically self-governing merely because a bureaucrat *routinely* accedes to his request.

The next problem arising from the above discussion is this. Many issues resolved by government employees cannot arguably be considered political. The most obvious instance is the decision by a traffic patrolman to give a motorist a trafic ticket. Another is a determination by a public university that its students will hope to take three years of a foreign language in order to be permitted to graduate. Another involves an announcement by a professor at that same university that his students will have to write three term papers, etc.[8] What follows from this is that when the individual persuades a bureaucrat to follow his wishes on a non-political matter, that person cannot be said to be *politically* self-governing. He may then be self-governing, but if he is, it is in a sphere other than that of politics (though perhaps just as important as the political). Thus, when the students at a public university convince the faculty that more courses dealing with Africa should be taught, they can certainly be considered at least slightly self-governing in one area of their lives, but they cannot be said to be self-governing politically. Likewise, the president of that university, though a "bureaucrat," is not politically self-governing merely because he decides it should offer Swahili.

Let us turn now to the judiciary. As we noted earlier, in some countries at least (the United States being the most prominent example), certain political issues are resolved by the courts. We already mentioned the cases declaring school segregation unconstitutional; and to these we can add the recent series of decisions in which the United States Supreme Court has said that the states are required to afford to persons accused of crime rigorous procedural safeguards from the time that they are taken into custody, the cases declaring it unconstitutional for the states to allow prayers to be said in public school classrooms, the opinions severely restricting the power of the states to ban literature which they deem obscene, etc. Even when the courts sustain a bill, they are resolving a political issue: viz., whether the state legislature or Congress had the power to enact that particular law.

Since most courts, even courts of original jurisdiction, do have the opportunity to resolve issues that can meaningfully be described as political, we can say that most members of the judiciary are by virtue of their position politically self-governing. We probably should exempt from this category the judges who man the magistrates courts and those who preside over the specialized courts for relatively minor disputes that have been set up in most American large cities (e.g., family and small claim courts). It also follows from our definition of the politically self-governing citizen that an individual who convinces a member of a court to vote as he wishes on a particular "political" issue before it is politically self-governing. It may not be so clear, however, who that person is in a particular case. Take, for example, a suit brought in a Federal District Court in Mississippi in which the court is asked to order the defendant school board to immediately integrate its public school system. The judge listens to all the arguments and then issues a decree granting the plaintiff's request. Does the issuance of the decree make the plaintiff a politically self-governing citizen if in fact the head of the local chapter of the National Association for the Advancement of Colored People had urged the plaintiff to sue and, moreover, the chapter was paying for his lawyer? If it is not the plaintiff who becomes politically active as a result of the decision, is it the chapter head — or is it the lawyer? This would probably depend on the facts. If the plaintiff sues merely as a favor to the chapter head, and if the lawyer argues the case merely to earn a fee, it is probably only the chapter head who is made politically self-governing. For one to be considered this under our definition, it must be his views which are among the reasons why the government official decides as he does; and in the circumstances I am postulating it is hard to say that either the lawyer or the plaintiff had any real views on the question of integration of the schools in the locality. But certainly the chapter head's beliefs *were* causally connected to the issuance of the order: the chapter head's position is analogous to that of the individual who convinces the interest group that in turn convinces a legislator — and we concluded earlier that that person was politically self-governing. On the other hand, if the lawyer and the plaintiff also wanted to see school integration and they were not functioning as the mere mouthpieces of the chapter head, they, too, could be said to be politically self-governing as a result of the judge's decree.

Of course, a plaintiff who wins a case involving issues that cannot reasonably be said to be political cannot be asserted to have become politically self-governing as a result of his victory. Thus one who successfully sues another driver for damages for injuries sustained as a result of the latter's negligence cannot be considered politically self-governing where the issues in the case were (a) was the other driver exceeding the speed limit and (b) were the plaintiff's windshield wipers working. Even if the issue were not factual but one of law, e.g., whether a negligent plaintiff can recover anything from an even-more-careless defendant, the result would probably not suffice to make the plaintiff politically self-governing. (However, if the state trial lawyers' association had been conducting a long campaign to allow a driver to win where he is careless but less so than the defendant, and this case were brought as a step in that campaign, the lawyer for the plaintiff could be considered to have attained this status.)

Criticisms of our definition of self-governing citizen

The above lengthy exercise in defining the ideal of a self-governing citizen of a representative democracy will doubtlessly be unsatisfactory to many anti-bureaucratic radicals. We can anticipate the following criticisms from their pens and/or those of others. These criticisms can be applied to our general definition of "self-governing citizen" but they will be phrased here only as criticism of our definition of "politically self-governing citizen."

A. Under the definition given, the degree to which individuals are politically self-governing may vary enormously. "Politically self-governing" individuals range all the way from the President of the United States and the Prime Minister of Great Britain to the citizen who gets the traffic commissioner of his town to agree that traffic lights should be installed at a nearby corner. They include the man who wins over ten senators and the man who proselytizes only one. They include the person who convinces a state legislator to vote for a bill doubling the amount the state spends on education and the one who persuades him to vote for a measure declaring Lincoln's birthday an official state holiday. They include the person who convinces a city councilman of the correctness of his views on five matters and the persons who influences him on only one.

There is nothing inherently absurd in defining politically self-governing in such a way that some can be more so than others. But many anti-bureaucratic radicals would insist that one is self-governing only when his power is equal to that of the other members of his group. Thus one of these thinkers seems to say that only in a *direct* democracy can men be genuinely self-governing. According to him, in the good society

> "Social decisions are made in a general assembly, where all members of the community have an opportunity to acquire the full measure of anyone who addresses them. They are in a position to absorb his attitudes and demeanor, to explore his motives as well as his ideas in a direct personal encounter and through thorough debate, face-to-face discussion and close inquiry. The execution of public tasks is left to committees, formed of voluteers or selected by lot. When specialized knowledge is required, the tasks are apportioned among technical groups, each member of which is subject to immediate recall. These committees and groups remain under constant public purview. Their work is limited exclusively to administrative tasks and they are answerable in every detail of their responsibilities to the assembly."[9]

Of course, no final answer can be given to the question of whether it is possible to define an individual as politically self-governing when under the definition itself there can be some who are more politically self-governing than he. What we are arguing about is a matter of definition, and there is no way to prove empirically than one definition is correct and another is incorrect. However, in addition to the fact that the definition we have given above is not self-contradictory or obviously ridiculous, there is another argument in its favor. If the anti-bureaucratic radicals employ it as the definition of their goal, their theory will gain in practicability what it loses in idealism. Whether or not it is impossible to set up a society in which every one has the same quantity of political power, it is almost certainly easier to create one in which all are self-governing but not equally so. To put this in another way, a community in which a man influences his councilman on five issues and his neighbor influences that representative on only one is a lot easier to imagine than one where they both influence him on the same number of issues of the same importance.

B. Somewhat related to the criticism of our definition set forth in "A," but perhaps more fundamental, is the following stricture (also one likely to come from anti-bureaucratic radicals with the views of the author of the above quote.) Under this definition, some people with really a very modest amount of political power are labelled as politically self-governing. For example, we have to categorize in this way the person who convinces a city councilman to vote for a measure altering the name of his street from "Broad" to "High." It must be confessed that this is the most troublesome result of our definition. However, this is an extreme case, and there is no real need to modify an otherwise satisfactory definition merely because it will produce awkward results in the odd situation. Furthermore, to change it to exclude from the class of political self-governing citizens persons such as those who convince the city to change a street name, we would have to qualify the word "issues" in our definition by the adjective "significant" or "important;" to adopt this course would be very unsatisfactory because of the vagueness of these modifiers. Also, the very fact that it can cover persons of this sort is in a sense one of its strengths, for it is another indication that it, unlike some of its superficially more attractive rivals, is not utopian on its face. (For example, suppose we were to say that one could not be a politically self-governing citizen unless at least one statute proposed by him were adopted each year by his local legislature. This would be defining our ideal that everyone should be self-governing in a way that would make it incapable of realization. To prove this, let us remind ourselves that, e.g., the Philadelphia City Council passes nowhere near two million laws per annum even though it has jurisdiction over this number of people.) So both because it admits that some men can be more politically self-governing than others and because it allows that an individual with a meager amount of political power can be fitted into this category, our definition does have the virtue of delimiting a goal whose realization does not strike one on first glance as beyond the realm of possibility.

C. The attentive reader will have noted that there is nothing in our definition that determines how long an individual who has in one way or another become politically self-governing can be said to retain this characteristic. This criticism is a telling one, and must be met by an attempt to add an appropriate clause to the definition.

To do this, let us proceed from a concrete situation. Suppose I convince my city councilman that he should vote against a proposed hike in a city tax. From what has preceded it follows that I can be considered politically self-governing, but for how long? Obviously, if I persuade him within a few months that he should vote for a modification of the zoning laws to allow more high-rise apartments to be built in the outlying areas of the city, I remain politically self-governing, at least for a little while. But what if, after my success with him on the tax issue, I rest on my laurels and stop prevailing upon the members of the governments with jurisdiction over me to make the decisions that I would like: at what point of time am I then to be colored politically impotent rather than politically self-governing? Obviously, it would be absurd to pick a particular point in time such as one year or two years after one has won over a bureaucrat or legislator and say that, in all cases where one has become politically self-governing, he must be said to have lost this characteristic after this date unless in the meanwhile he successfully pressures another official or the same official again. All that we can honestly do is use legal language to the effect that one who has become politically self-governing retains this status for a "reasonable time." And what is a reasonable time will vary with many factors: e.g., the significance of the issue or issues on which he won, the number of persons with decision-making power he won over, the number of the issues on which he has been successful in the past, etc. Thus, for example, one who convinces five United States senators to vote for a bill expanding the nation's public housing program can not only be considered more politically self-governing than a person who prevails upon his city councilman to vote for a change in the name of a street; but, moreover, all other things being equal, he can be said to keep this status for a longer period of time. In a sense, the pleasant aftertaste of a significant and sweeping victory lasts longer than that from a relatively trivial and limited one; and it would be erroneous to ignore this truth when it comes to framing our definitions.

To summarize this chapter, we have found that one of the major goals of the current anti-bureaucratic left is the development of a self-governing citizenry. Most of our time has been spent formulating a definition of who is a politically self-governing citizen, explaining some terms it employs, using some hypothetical cases to further clarify it, and discussing a few of the more sensible criticisms that could be levied against it. It is now time to see in more detail how these anti-statist radicals would reorganize society so as to achieve this aim.

FOOTNOTES TO CHAPTER III

1. Jacobs and Landau, *op. cit.,* p. 154.
2. *Ibid.,* p. 155.
3. *See Ibid.,* pp. 155-56.
4. *Self-Government in Industry,* 5th ed. (London: G. Bell & Sons, 1920), p. 185.
5. "Post-Stalinist Shock", *Nation,* 183-90, August 4, 1956.
6. *Essays in Social Theory* (London: Oldbourne, 1962), p. 99.
7. The shippers, railroads and airlines have good relations with the independent regulatory commissions that supposedly govern them in the public interest, while the Corps of Engineers wants to remain free to decide what rivers it shall dredge and what harbors it shall deepen.
8. Note, however, that issues which would normally be considered as non-political may in fact be highly political under certain circumstances. When New York City, to end an emotion-ridden teachers strike which the Negro community viewed as racist in motivation, agreed to keep the schools open an hour or so longer each day so that the teachers could make up their lost wages, the question of how long the schools should be open was certainly political.
9. Bookchin, Murray, "Post-Scarcity Anarchy," on p. 329 of Silberman, Henry (ed.) *American Radical Thought: The Libertarian Tradition* (Lexington, Mass.: D. C. Heath, 1970). C. George Benello and Dimitrious Roussopolous agree that a par ticipatory democracy must be a direct democracy. See p. 5 of their Introduction to the book edited by them entitled *The Case for Participatory Democracy* (New York: Grossman, 1971).

IV

PARTICIPATORY DEMOCRACY: A BLUEPRINT AND ITS POTENTIAL FOR SUCCESS

Having just explored various aspects of the ideal of a self-governing citizenry, a citizen body whose members will severally have a share in determing the policy that affects their lives, we must now first see whether the decentralist socialism the anti-bureaucratic radicals propound will even in theory make likely the attainment of this ideal. To do this we must, of course, become clearer than we have heretofore been about the outlines of the politico-economic system that we are calling "decentralized socialism" or "participatory democracy." The difficulty with doing this is that few if any of the diverse individuals and groups that we are lumping together under this label of "anti-bureaucratic radical" provide us with anything near a complete blueprint of what a participatory democracy would look like. They usually talk in vague generalities such as

"The humanist does not say: 'We shall accept this dismal house of bondage and try to redecorate it.' He says rather: 'We shall insist on the priority of man's freedom and ground our social invention in the ethic of the social contract freely made.' The primary task of the humanist is to describe and help to realize those political acts through which the power of the central authoritarian monolith can be broken and the political life of man reconstituted on the basis of the associational, democratic non-exclusive community."[1]

Only when they hit upon a topic close to their hearts do these radicals get down to specifics. For example, the Negroes who advocate black control of the ghetto concentrate almost entirely on what should be done with the political and economic institutions in neighborhoods such as this and almost totally ignore how the white world outside should be restructured. White university students, both in the United States and in Europe, are mainly interested in the problem of how much authority they should have within the university. And black American university students are primarily concerned with the extent of their right to shape the university's Afro-American Studies program. It should be emphasized that there is absolutely no intention here to "blame" these various groupings within the anti-statist left for concentrating almost entirely upon the reorganization of one particular aspect of society. After all, most of them are primarily action-oriented and thus have little time or energy to relate other than in a general way the reform that is their central concern to other changes in the social order.

However, we can, by projecting from the specific changes suggested by various members of the anti-bureaucratic left, draft a blueprint of the "participatory democracy" they believe should be created, among other reasons, to give the individual real control over his own life. What in essence we are doing is pasting together their sketches of their particular rooms to construct a diagram of the entire house. Obviously, some of them would feel uncomfortable living there; for it places too much emphasis for them on representative as opposed to direct democracy. But the majority would conclude that its atmosphere is much less oppressive and much warmer than that of the dwellings they presently inhabit.

The blueprint provides that an elective body representative of a city neighborhood between, say, five thousand and fifty thousand population (there is no agreement on any particular figure) would be given the authority to operate the libraries, the schools, the public works, anti-poverty, recreational and street maintenance programs, and the health, police, fire, sanitation and welfare services that are located or carried out within the neighborhood. Thus Norman Mailer demanded, when he sought the Democratic nomination for mayor of New York City in 1969, that each neighborhood should run its own police and fire department, schools, parks and garbage services.[2] And the community organizer Tom Hayden tried to organize a referendum in Berkeley, California, to set up community control of the police.[3] As we noted in Chapter I, many American blacks insist that community schools must be managed by the black community; and have added ghetto control of the police in the ghetto to their list.[4]

In the factory or office, not only would the enterprise not be conducted for profit, but a committee of the workers would have the right to resolve questions of production, price, wages, hours and conditions of labor. The SDS's Port Huron Statement says that "the economic experience is so personally decisive that the individual must share in its full determination."[5] (156) And the French student leader Jacques Sauvageot not only calls for student power but for workers' control of the factories. As he said in an interview held in Spring of 1968,

> "The population and the workers must be reassured. We must propose to them, not another government, but the effective power of the workers in their factories. [Workers' control means] the control of firms by the workers . . . We no longer speak of "soviets" (The Russian word for "committee") because the word is old fashioned. But that is what we are really talking about when we refer to control."[6]

The type of factory, etc., management described in the first sentence of this paragraph seems to be what is called for by these demands.

To continue with our blueprint of the society characterized

by decentralized socialism, in the university and high school students and faculty would have equal representation on committees that were charged with approving courses and setting requirements. (This is the very demand the students and faculty at the author's college who conceive of themselves as radicals are making for the governance of the college.) In the area of the consumption of goods, the large, privately owned department store or supermarket would be replaced by a cooperative owned by the people living in the area it served and managed by a board of directors they elected. The anti-bureaucratic radicals have not wasted many words discussing the problem of how the distribution of goods and services should be organized, except to call for community control of services such as health and sanitation which at present are to some extent publicly furnished. However, the formation by radical groups of "co-ops" in poor neighborhoods or in areas inhabited by students and "street people" indicates that some participatory democrats do favor the "co-op" way of administering the distribution of goods and services. (Some others might say that the relevant neighborhood government should administer stores and supermarkets). Finally little is said in the writings of the anti-bureaucratic left about the role of the city, state or national political systems.[7] The quotes from Murray Bookchin in the last chapter and Carl Oglesby in this indicate, however, that many of them would prefer to relegate these to a minimal role in regulating producers and consumers; i.e., that they would favor little if any control of neighborhood governments, workers' councils, consumers' councils, etc. by higher levels of government. In other words, in our blueprint of participatory democracy, major policy decisions emanate from these small scale organs rather than from metropolitan regional or national governments.[8]

Does this blueprint even provide the *potential* for creating a self-governing citizenry? That is, does the society it sketches make it simpler than it is at present for the average man to participate in shaping the rules to which he is subject—forgetting for the moment about whether he is likely *in practice* to take advantage if any increased opportunities for such participation it may furnish him? To answer this, let us look first at one of the features of participatory democracy that we noted quickly a few paragraphs ago: neighborhood control over local expenditures of anti-poverty funds. Jones, a hypothetical resident of a slum area, urgently desires that the funds from the American government's "war on poverty" to which his neighborhood is entitled be used to subsidize a pre-school education program for three and four year old children. Assume, first of all, that it is the federal Office of Economic Opportunity in Washington that has the power to determine whether this money will be spent in this community for this purpose or some other, say a training program for unemployed youth. (In fact, this particular issue would probably be resolved by a city or neighborhood group even at present. But the following discussion of what would happen were it decided by a federal agency at present is of value simply because so much policy *is* made on this level.) Jones will for practical purposes not be able to sway any of the relevant decision-makers. The chances are that he cannot afford a trip to Washington or that he will be afraid to go, even if he has a few dollars saved up. Suppose he does make the trip: what are his chances of convincing even one policy-maker and thus becoming "politically self-governing" as we defined that term in the last chapter? An honest answer would have to be "very little." If he walks into office headquarters and asks for an interview with someone he'll probably be asked to see a minor bureaucrat with minimal authority, as those officials with the real power will probably be too busy for one reason or another to talk to him. Even if one can spare a moment or two, that person will have no incentive whatsoever to pay him any serious attention. The official is not dependent on Jones' vote for continuing in office nor is there any reasonable chance that Jones will be able to convince his Congressman to "make trouble" for the program. And so he will nod politely, usher Jones out of the office in ten minutes, and five minutes after that forget everything Jones has said. What will happen, then, if Jones, sensing failure at the Office of Economic Opportunity, decides to pay a visit to his Congressman. Nine chances out of ten that individual will be busy and so Jones will be given an appointment with a harried legislative assistant who will probably fail to pass Jones' message on to his "boss." Even if he does get to see the solon, the chat will probably not result in swinging him over to his views in case he is initially opposed, simply because the Congressman has a couple of hundred thousand voters in his district which means that he will not be worried about alienating one rather ordinary one. Of course, Jones could forget about the trip to Washington and write a letter to the Office of Economic Opportunity. But then all the action he would get is a letter typed by a secretary and signed by her in an official's name thanking him for taking the trouble to write.

On the other hand, let us suppose that the body with the power to decide how anti-poverty money is to be allocated in Jones' community is a ten-man group elected by its ten thousand adults. The office of the group will be in the neighborhood and so it will be an easy matter for Jones to pay a visit after work or on a Saturday morning. The members of the group are not likely to have any assistants whom they can interpose between themselves and an interview with Jones. Moreover, Jones will be less afraid to demand a personal audience with one of the members of the board simply because they are his neighbors and come from a similar socioeconomic class. And when the interview is granted, the board member is less likely than the congressman or the OEO official to mentally ignore Jones' point of view simply because Jones is one of ten thousand constituents rather than one of

a couple of hundred thousand. In fact Jones' chances of prevailing upon a member of the board and thus of becoming
"politically self-governing" are rather good, and certainly infinitely better than they would be were the decision to be
made in the capital.

Turning now to the factory, we find that the worker has
little if any power to determine the way in which his working hours are spent. It is true that he is probably a union
member and that the union will annually or biennially
wrestle with management over questions of wages, hours and
working conditions. It is also true that the officials of his
local and national are elected by him and his fellow members and also that any particular grievance he may have may
well be taken up with management by a union official. So
a stranger unschooled in these affairs would assume that he
has a fairly good chance to become self-governing at work
by getting in touch with a union leader and converting him
to his point of view on wages, hours, etc. But in reality the
American union, at least, is a little oligarchy not responsive
to the membership individually. And, more importantly, the
union in any case usually has no say on questions of production, distribution, etc.

If all questions confronting the factory had to be decided
by a works council representing just the workers in that enterprise, the individual worker would clearly have more chance
to be self-governing in the economic or "vocational" sphere.
For one thing, his councillor would share decision-making
power on more issues (e.g., production) than does the union
leader of today, and so the number of questions on which he
could try to convince the former would be greater. In addition, each councillor would have fewer constituents, and thus
be more likely to pay attention to the views of each individual constituent, than does the average labor leader who
participates in the collective bargaining process. (It should
not be forgotten that these labor leaders are often chosen
not by a particular factory, but on a city-wide, company-wide,

or even an industry-wide level.) Moreover, most union officials adopt a "middle-class" way of living and speaking once elevated to union office, and as a consequence some ordinary members are afraid to approach them. The works councillor, however, would have the time to spend part of the day working in the shop with his constituents, and thus they would have plenty of opportunity to contact him and no reason to be afraid to take such a step.

At present, it is frequently true that the high school or college student has no say in determining what courses will be offered by his institution. In the case of the high school, the curriculum is set by the principal and some members of his staff who, in turn, have their hands tied by requirements promulgated by the state (e.g., so many years of American history, so many years of gym, etc.). In the university, the course offerings are formally determined by a faculty committee on courses and/or the faculty as a whole. In practice, however, the faculty members can teach more or less what they please, especially if they are willing to submit to the faculty committee's rather lengthy course descriptions in sextuplicate so that the committee can go through the formality of ratifying their wishes. On both high school and college levels, especially the former, most students would not dream of even asking that such and such a subject be given or that such and such a course be dropped but accept what appears in the catalog as God's will. In fact, a high school pupil who made such a request might be suspended from school. Some of the more liberal colleges have recently begun the practice of allowing one or two students to sit as voting members of the faculty course committee, but this is clearly tokenism where the students are outnumbered four or five to one.

The situation could be radically altered if the college or school course committee were to have fifty percent student membership. Each student could then go to his committeeman to ask that the latter make a request at the next committee meeting that such and such a course be given. If he were successful in convincing him, he would then be "educationally self-governing." He would have no reason to be afraid of speaking to the student representative who, after all, would be a fellow student. Likewise, the representative would have good reason to listen to him respectfully simply because the opposition of the student and his friends might well mean defeat at the next election.

Finally, most Americans, and now many Europeans as well, do as good deal of their weekly shopping at a supermarket, which is usually a link a nationwide or region-wide chain. In general, we buy from what is laid out on the shelves in front of us at the prices set by the regional office of the supermarket. To a considerable extent then, what we buy in the way of food and the amount we have to pay for it is now determined for us by others, and this is true whether we shop at the local A & P or at the Northeast Moscow branch of the Food Distribution Agency of the Russian Socialist Federated Socialist Republic. Of course, the A & P shoppers in toto or in a particular area have *as a group* a fair amount of say over what appears on the food counters: the much-vaunted sovereignty of the consumer under capitalism is not a complete myth. If, as a group, they don't want to buy fish, either the price of fish will fall rapidly or the A & P will cease selling fish. If the A & P's Board of Directors knows that they want to buy more sugarless soda, more sugarless soda is likely to appear in the beverage department. If a particular A & P is located in a Jewish neighborhood, the manager will see that the store has an adequate supply of gefilte fish and fresh rye bread; if in an Italian area, that it sells plenty of veal and pasta, etc. But the only power the *individual* shopper at the local A & P has is to choose between Florida and California oranges, between brown bread and white. If he goes to the manager to ask him to stock a bread made with stone-ground flour or to reduce the price of apples he is likely at best to be met with a jovial shake of the head.

On the other hand, suppose ownership and control of the local A & P were to be switched to a general-purpose neighborhood government or to a cooperative in which all the residents were members. The board of directors would then be elected by the residents and, presumably, live in the neighborhood themselves. It would be very easy, then, for a neighbor who had complaints about service or who wanted the store to sell a new kind of bread to make his wishes known to a board member The board member would be likely to listen to him with attention simply because he would be one of a relatively small number of constituents. For this reason, he should not have too much trouble getting his stone-ground bread or an increase in the number of shopping carts that have a place for seating children.

To sum up, we can easily explain why the proposals of the anti-bureaucratic radicals for "decentralized socialism," i.e., for transferring decision-making power from the national, state and local to the neighborhood level and from private management to the people, are potentially productive of a situation in which, unlike now, each person has a real say in shaping the rules determining how he lives. The transfer of prerogatives already public from the center to work places and communities will, in the first place, make it physically and fiscally simpler to contact one or more of the men legally responsible for making the pertinent decisions. As we saw, for example, it will be much less complex in every way for Jones, our slum-dweller who wants a pre-school program, to get in touch with a member of a neighborhood poverty agency than with a Washington employee of the Office of Economic Opportunity. Likewise, the same example shows that this transfer of power will produce decision-makers who are of the same socio-economic class as their constituents, and this in turn will make it psychologically easier for the latter to try to convince them of the soundness of their views. Decentralization also will mean a reduction in the number of constituents persons in authority deal with, and, consequently, an increase in the time they have available to spend with each individual voter and in the motivation they have for considering his point of view with respect. Certainly the member of the local poverty agency will find it more feasible than the average member of the United States House of Representatives to set aside several hours a day for chats with his constituents — and he may well conclude that it is dangerous to ignore completely the ideas of any one of these men. And the assignment of the right to manage factories and stores from private hands to bodies representative of the workers and neighborhoods will mean that policy-making has been taken out of the hands of a group of persons who are perceived as arbitrary, overworked, physically remote, of a distant social class, and under no obligation to those directly affected by their dictates. So we must admit that the anti-bureaucratic radicals have been logical by calling for reforms which do help pave the way for the man or woman who wishes to become more self-governing, and which are thus in theory conducive to the realization of one of their crucial ideas. Their political philosophy may be flawed in some ways — but certainly not in this particular and crucial respect.

FOOTNOTES TO CHAPTER IV

1. Oglesby, Carl — "Two Issues Revised," p. 354 of Silberman, Henry (ed.) *American Radical Thought: The Libertarian Tradition* (Lexington, Mass.: D. C. Heath and Co.).

2. Mailer's article on which this speech is based, "Why Are We in New York," appeared in *New York Times Magazine*, May 18, 1969, p. 101.

3. See his *At Issue: Peaceful Change or Civil War*, New York *Times*, March 9, 1971, p. 37.

4. See e.g. the Black Panther Petition for Neighborhood control of the Police, p. 428 of Cook, Terrence and Morgan, Patrick (eds.), *Participatory Democracy* (San Francisco: Canfield Press, 1971). Cook and Morgan's chapter one is a very good introduction to the pros and cons of participatory democracy.

5. This quote can be found on p. 156 of Jacobs and Landau, *op. cit.*

6. Quoted on p. 22 of Cohn-Bendit, Daniel, et al: *The French Student Revolt: The Leaders Speak* (New York: Hill and Wang, 1968).

7. Alan Altshuler is one exception. See pp. 154-189 of his *Community Control* (New York: Pegasus, 1970).

8. It must be noted that some persons who might identify themselves as anti-bureaucratic radicals call for a growth in the power of the central government simultaneously with the changes we have been discussing in this chapter. Thus Yale Law Professor Charles Reich is viewed by many as eschewing radical reform of institutions in favor of radical reform of consciousness. However in an article entitled *Issues For a New Society* (*New York Times,* March 9, 1971 p. 37) he says that "In a complex society, it is foolish to pretend that democracy is satisfied by a once a year election day. People must be able to 'vote' every day by expressing their values on the job, as newly aware consumers, in many kinds of groups and organizations, and in a variety of public hearings." However these words follow by only one paragraph this assertion: "The first affirmative requirement of a new society is a system of planning, allocation and design. Today there is no control over what any organization may invest, produce, use up, distribute. The need for planning has been obvious since before the New Deal, but we have refused to see it."

V

PARTICIPATORY DEMOCRACY
AND THE SELF-GOVERNING CITIZEN:
WORKS COUNCILS

It is all very well to say that the anti-bureaucratic radicals' call for political, economic, and social decentralization is potentially productive of greater self-determination for the individual. However, the more important question is: will it do so *in practice?* The reason why asking about the theory will not really give us any clue about the practice is simple. All the considerations of the last chapter really demonstrated was that the average man might well find it simpler to become self-governing under these reforms, but they did not and could not indicate anything about whether he would grasp this improved opportunity. That is, they indicated that under these changes he probably *could* gain greater control of his future, and not that he *would,* and there is clearly a great deal of difference between these two assertions. Potential political and other forms of power may, for a wide variety of reasons, never be actualized. To take just one obvious example, decision-making power about a pre-school program in the neighborhood may have been shifted from a Washington bureaucrat to a neighborhood agency, but the residents of the neighborhood may just be too lethargic or apathetic to put pressure on the members of the new organization even though the latter are socially and geographically accessible.

71

What must be done in this chapter is to start to bring the theoretical considerations of the last down to earth. That is, we shall be concerned here with the problem of whether the individual would *in fact* be likely to have a meaningful voice in the running of the local, potentially easy-to-influence institutions proposed by the decentralist socialists of today. To anticipate, this chapter will study factory works councils: our next will consider other reforms designed to make it easier for men to govern themselves.

There is, unfortunately, little in the writings of the anti-bureaucratic radicals that is useful in helping us determine whether their proposals will in actuality create a situation in which men draft for themselves the policy that affects them. They seem to follow the path of Owen, Marx, Engels and Kropotkin and merely assume that the members of the human race are basically good, intelligent, and concerned about others. For example, to repeat a sentence already quoted from the Port Huron Statement of the American SDS: "We regard *men* as infinitely precious and possessed of unfulfilled capacities for reason, freedom and love. . . . Men have unrealized potential for self-cultivation, self-direction, self-understanding, and creativity."[1] Likewise, the problem with men of today is institutional rather than inherent: they are but the prisoners of a wicked social system which prevents them from becoming all that they can. For example, "the American political system is not the democratic model of which its glorifiers speak. In actuality it frustrates democracy by confusing the individual citizen, paralyzing policy discussion, and consolidating the irresponsible power of military and business interests."[2] The assumption behind the Port Huron Stateement is that once the "para-fascist" American political system is replaced by local institutions which make theoretically possible "democracy of individual participation,"[3] men are so other-regarding and so reasonable that this "democracy of individual participation" will flourish. But that it would in reality be likely to bloom once reforms of this nature have been completed is not at all self-evident; and so it will be our purpose in this chapter and the next to test this thesis.

But, the reader will doubtlessly now ask, how will it be possible for us to indicate in any meaningful way the accuracy of the decentralist socialist view that the replacement of the large scale capitalism and state socialism of today by small scale political and economic institutions not operated for a profit will *in fact* give the individual a greater role in shaping the rules that govern him. The good society of anti-bureaucratic radicalism is still to come; so how is it possible to come up with anything more than an uneducated guess about how it will work? The answer is that though this society is a long way from realization, there have been set up on a small scale in our present social order a few institutions which would be much more common there and which would be the vehicles for the individual's playing this enhanced role. These institutions include, for example, "works councils" in the factories of certain countries, neighborhood agencies to determine the use of anti-poverty funds in the United States, and faculty committees to participate in the governing of the university. However they function in practice, they do in theory give the workers in these enterprises, the poor in these areas, and the faculty in these universities a say in the drafting of factory, anti-poverty, and university policy respectively; and would certainly be carried over and expanded in good society of the anti-bureaucratic radicals (except that students would be added to the faculty committees in significant number). Whether they do in actuality give the workers, etc. this say would thus seem to be of relevance to those interested in the question of whether they would have the same effect under a full-fledged system of decentralized socialism: for example, if they were successes in this respect now, our guess to the effect that they and other democratic communities of similar size would be so then would at least have the virtue of being an educated one, though it is admittedly doubtful that such an assertion could receive the label of "scientific prediction."

Let us turn to the factory works council to determine whether it has given the workers in the firms where it is to be found a share in shaping the rules which govern their life at work. The works council is an institution probably unknown to the English or American reader, but it has been set up in quite a few European countries, including France, Belgium, Austria, West Germany and Yugoslavia. Basically, a works council is a body elected by the workers in a plant to share to a greater or lesser degree in the management of that plant. The council may be set up in a state-owned enterprise, as in Yugoslavia, or a privately owned concern, as in West Germany. It may have purely advisory powers, it may have the right to veto management proposals in certain areas, or it may have the sole say in framing certain types of policy. Obviously, the possible variations in council structure and/or function are almost infinite; but whatever particular shape it may take and whatever the political reasons for its creation it is a device which, as we saw in the last chapter, *can* lead the worker to have a greater share in factory decision-making. *Whether it has had this result in practice will be the concern of the remainder of this chapter.* To the extent that the answer is yes, we can say that the analogous organizations which would certainly be an important feature of decentralist socialism would produce a similar result and thus help achieve one of the most cherished goals of anti-statist radicalism.

In this paper, the works councils that will be studied with the above purpose in mind are those which have been set up in Yugoslavia and West Germany. (However, we shall also refer briefly to the Polish councils.) It is these councils which in theory at least are the most far-reaching experiments with workers' control of industry and it is they which have been most intensively observed by social scientists of various persuasions. In Yugoslavia, for example, the council can determine what the enterprise will produce and (within limits set by law) the prices that it can charge for what it produces. The council also has the right to decide about the organization of the plan and the establishment of vacation schedules, to allocate jobs within the firm, to run the firm's recreational and welfare facilities, to hire all employees except the plant director and the higher administrative and professional staff, and, in conjunction with the relevant unit of local government, to dismiss the plant director. Every enterprise is to have a works council which varies in size from five to one hundred, depending upon the size of the plant. The councillors serve for two year periods and the council itself elects a managing board, which is to run the plant in accordance with its directions. The plant director is to be responsible for the day-to-day operation of the plant in accordance with the decision of the council and the board.

In West Germany, the basic law regarding works councils is entitled the *Betriebsverfassungsgesetz* of 1951 (which will henceforth be called the BVG. Incidentally, the BVG must be distinguished from the *Mitbestimmungsgesetz* of 1951, which is the act requiring employee representation on the management organs of steel and mining firms.) In each of the factories which is subject to it, there is to be a works council (*Betriebsrat*) whose members are to be chosen by all the workers in the factory in biennial elections. The *Betriebsräte* have the following statutory powers, but may be granted additional prerogatives (or may obtain material benefits for their constituents over and above those appearing in the relevant collective bargaining agreement) by concluding, with the management of their respective firms, "plant agreements" which accord them such extra powers, etc. First of all, they are to supervise the operation of labor laws and collective bargaining agreements and to discuss employee complaints with the management. Moreover, the *Betriebsrat* has the right to participate equally with management in the making of decisions concerning the time that the work day is to begin and end, vacation and rest pause schedules, vocational training, works rules, the establishment and administration of certain plant welfare facilities (e.g., health centers, vacation homes, emergency funds), and the time, place and method of wage and salary payments. It has, as well, the power to appeal to a conciliation board in the event that it and the employer are unable to come to an agreement in a particular case involving one or more of these questions and he has disregarded its wishes.

When any hiring or transfer of employees takes place, the management must notify the *Betriebsrat* in advance. If this hiring or transfer, in the opinion of the council, (1) violates a law or a collective bargaining agreement, (2) involves nepotism or racial or political discrimination, or (3) threatens the peace of the plant, it may appeal to a labor court, which is then to issue a decision that is binding upon all parties. Likewise, the council must be notified beforehand whenever any employee is discharged. In addition, when management decides to transfer the plant to another area, to close the plant or a large division thereof, to merge with another concern, or to introduce new labor methods, the *Betriebsrat* may protest if the proposed action will operate to the disadvantage of the work force. If no compromise can be reached with the employer, it — or he — may have a special board act as a mediator. The decisions of this board are not binding upon him, but if he rejects its proposals and if, as a result, some employees are dismissed, they can sue him for damages and recover, unless the court finds that his action was economically justified.[4]

Before we turn to the actual functioning of these German and Yugoslav councils, one more point must be mentioned. It is obvious that if certain things are true, the councils cannot be said to give the workers much of a voice in the running of the plant. Thus, if the works councils did little or came under the control of an individual or a small group of individuals on or off the council (e.g., the employer, the director of the plant), it would be hard to say that their presence increased the role of the workers in formulating policy for the enterprise. The same would be true if the councils insulated themselves from whatever worker pressure was forthcoming — irrespective of whether or not elitist behavior made their decisions more or less rational. And, finally, if the workers are more or less oblivious to the council and its various doings it likewise cannot be said that this institution has made them more self-governing. It is for these reasons that our study of works councils will concentrate on these points: viz., the vitality and independence of the councils, their responsiveness to their electorate, and the degree of worker interest in their operation.

On point number 1, the activity and independence of the councils, the students of the Yugoslavian experiment are split, some holding that the council leaves most decision-making to the plant director or some plant official and others asserting that it really exercises its statutory prerogatives. One observer in the former camp went to a meeting which he admitted was lively and productive of suggestions. However, he felt that the council had no decision-making power, for those who presided at the session made no attempt to find out how it felt about any specific question. No proposition was actually put to a vote though in a few cases the secretary of the council summed up what he thought was the sense of the conclave. The writer concluded that the council could expect to be consulted but not to have its opinions respected.[5]

An American sociologist was permitted to make a content analysis of the minutes of the council of another firm. The minutes showed that while the twenty-six councillors were quite talkative, they made only nine decisions during the course of the year. The council chairman made thirty-eight while the director of the plant was responsible for sixty-six. In this firm, the director clearly ruled the roost; and that individual frankly admitted that the council had never rejected any suggestion that management considered important.[6]

The Yugoslavs themselves have at times stated that for

one reason or another some of their works councils do not exercise their powers. The journal *Borba* confessed that in some factories the councils adopt an almost blank balance sheet, leaving it to the director to fill in the details.[7] And another paper noted a director to whom the existence of the plant's council was but a mere formality and who allowed it no right but the right to vote.[8]

But it would be extremely unfair to the Yugoslavs to assert that it is only the exceptional council that is exercising its powers, and there is little doubt that a good number do really participate in the management of the firm. Thus at one session of a council, the plant's chief engineer made proposals suggesting that much of the plant's machinery be rehabilitated. These recommendations were accepted in principle only, and it was agreed that the council should consider at a later date the many ideas about this topic that the councillors themselves had furnished at the meeting. Toward the end of the session, one woman representative requested that two new employees in the firm's kitchen get more pay than the director wished them to have, and her proposals were adopted.[9] One book sums the position of the Yugoslav councils up this way: " . . . the meaningfulness of worker management varied from enterprise to enterprise. Some workers' councils visited by the author were obviously in control of their operation and doing an efficient job. Others were either not determining important management questions or were doing it inadequately."[10]

As for West Germany, the most thorough study of the nation's works councils (*Betriebsräte*) indicates that most of these are exercising at least some of the rights guaranteed to theem by the BVG, though those in large companies are more active than those in small firms. The study covered thirteen concerns, five of which were "small," employing fewer than two hundred persons, five of which were "medium-sized," employing between two hundred and five hundred workers, and five of which were "large," employing over five hundred individuals. In the "social matters" covered by the BVG, e.g., the determination of the time that the work day is to begin and end, the fixing of rules governing behavior in the plant and the time place and method of wage payments, the drafting of the vacation schedule and the operation of the factory welfare establishments, councils in both the large and small firms had considerable say, though only the former fully exercised their right of co-determination — i.e., equal say with management.[11] In the large and medium plants, the employer would not think of firing an employee before the *Betriebsrät* had been notified, and even in the smaller firms the employer frequently took this step.[12] And in all thirteen concerns the councils were notified in advance when management proposed to hire a new worker. However, the book refers to another study which found that this practice was much less frequent in the nation's smaller concerns.[13] Likewise, in the larger factories but usually not in the smaller the council and employer had entered into supplementary agreements which extended the powers granted to the council.[14]

Another book emphasized that the *Betriebsräte* are very active in getting wages for their workers which are higher than those set in the collective bargaining agreement covering the firm. As a result of bargaining by works councils in factories covered by the metal workers union, the workers there who were paid by the hour received on the average sixteen percent more per hour than the sum provided for in the union-employers-association contract. This volume also noted that the councils have a good deal of influence in the administration of the welfare facilities that have been established in their respective enterprises.[15]

I myself interviewed a few years ago the council chairman or vice-chairman of five large plants located in the city of Düsseldorf. What I found certainly indicates that the *Betriebsräte* in large firms do in fact play the role envisaged for them by the BVG. My first visit was to an automobile manufacturing concern which had just been purchased by a large, well known German automobile company. This council, like all the others I studied, really does have joint say with management over questions such as rest pause schedules, the time of the beginning and end of the working day, etc. No one can work overtime unless the council has given its consent. The *Betriebsrät* helps operate the company canteen, employee life insurance fund, and a credit union. More importantly, it has concluded several agreements with management which give its constituents a salary twenty-five percent greater than that accorded them by the collective bargaining contract and which permit employees who do unpleasant tasks to receive a bonus and to obtain free work clothes. It is informed about all proposed hirings and firings, and in some cases its protest has saved the job of an employee the firm was about to discharge. When the plant was purchased by the large concern it threatened to exercise its legal right to appeal to a special mediation board if the plant personnel were seriously hurt by the merger, and, as a result, the new owner did not discharge anyone. Finally, this council helps draft the rules regulating the behavior of the worker while at work (e.g., those telling him where he can and cannot smoke) and reprimands those employees who violate these rules, who come to work too late, or who take excessively long coffee breaks.

Another firm whose council chairman I spoke to manufacturers steel tubes for export. The housing committee of this council decides which workers will be able to rent apartments in company-built houses, while the social committee supervises the operation of the canteen. The council as a whole can have urgent repairs in the factory made at the company's expense. No employee can be discharged for disciplinary reasons without the approval of an eight-member commission composed of one employer representative from each of the parent concern's four companies in the Düsseldorf area and of one representative from each of the works councils of these four companies. This council entered into an agreement with the employer as a result of which some employees found their paychecks increased by as much as fifty percent. The councils in the three other firms I saw also had concluded pacts with management which gave the workers significant additional rights, e.g., free work clothing, Christmas and vacation bonuses, and discounts on the consumer goods produced in these concerns. At least one of these councils has convinced management not to discharge workers who were guilty of certain petty thefts.

The problem of whether the works council acts as an oligarchy which is not sensitive to the desires of its constituents is likewise not capable of a simple answer. In Yugoslavia some councils at times ignore the demands of the work forces. A few of them, contrary to law, close their meetings to nonmembers while others do not inform the workers of what they are doing or do not convene the legally required number of plant personnel assemblies.[16] A questionnaire circulated by *Borba* showed that only fifty-six percent of the workers who completed the form said that their works council had disclosed to them what it was trying to accomplish.[17] And the Yugoslavs themselves have admitted that many works councils have become elites interested solely in their own welfare and paying no attention to the views of the ordinary worker.[18]

But there are many Yugoslav councils which have showed themselves very responsive to their constituents. During those periods when Yugoslav councils were free to set wages, wages rose rapidly. For example, in 1961, productivity increased only three percent but personal income rose twenty-three percent.[19] This phenomenon, whose implications will be discussed in greater detail in a later chapter, obviously cannot be greeted with unrestrained approval by the advocates of decentralization and workers' control; but it does indicate that some Yugoslav councils do pay attention to the wishes of the voters. And we already have solid evidence in the form of the plant agreements that the German *Betriebsräte* have concluded with management that these institutions frequently act with the good of their electorate at heart. In addition, an event at one of the firms I visited is additional testimony that some councils are concerned with the views of the ordinary worker. In that plant there is one *Betriebsrät* member for every four hundred and fifty workers. It was found that, as a result of this, most employees had no contact at all with their *Betriebsrat,* representative. To remedy this situation, the quarterly plant personnel meeting was replaced by a system under which each of the ninety divisions of the firm elects an individual who informs the council of the desires of his division. It goes without saying that a *Betriebsrät* simply desirous of furthering its own interests would never have taken such a step!

The most obvious obstacle to the use of the works council as a device to increase worker participation in factory management is the possible lack of ordinary worker interest in its activities. It does appear that the reaction of the ordinary employee to the doings of the council is one of almost total unconcern. Various studies of German councils have indicated that the workers have no awareness of the concrete tasks these bodies are supposed to perform: most of them are fuzzily aware that it is supposed to represent their interests but few have any knowledge of the ways in which it is supposed to carry out this duty.[20] A chairman of a *Betriebsrät* in a leading Rhineland light metal firm told a correspondent of the *Times* of London: "The workers in our place are really not interested in their works council. They come to us quickly enough if they have a pay question or a dispute about hours with the management. They are concerned only with what they can get out of it, I suppose. I think all works council chairmen have had the same experience."[21] And when quarterly meetings of the plant personnel to discuss the *Betriebsrät*'s activities are held in the nation's mining and iron and steel firms, they will be well attended only if they are held on work days. At one such meeting, convened on a Sunday, only one-fourth of the work force of the mine was present.[22]

At four of the five firms I visited, I did not uncover much

one way or the other about whether or not the workers paid attention to the conduct of their *Betriebsrät*. (It is true that about 76% of the workers do vote in the council elections, but it is by now a truism to say that voting is consistent with a high degree of apathy.) At the fifth firm, only 15% of the work force came to the plant personnel meetings when it was the custom to hold these between the morning and afternoon shifts. This certainly indicates that they do not worry much about the activities of the council, and its vice-chairman explicitly confirmed this.

There exists less information about the interest shown by the Yugoslav workers who are not works councillors about the functioning of the council. The percentage of workers participating in council elections is very high here as in West Germany, but once again that proves very little. One observer found that when meetings of the entire firm were held to discuss the activities of the councils, the non-members of the council tended not to participate.[23] And a student of the short-lived Polish experiment with workers control of industry discovered almost no concern with the doings of their council on the part of the workers in the factory he studied in depth.[24] Of course, the existence of apathy in Poland and Yugoslavia should not surprise us: if the relatively well-educated German worker ignores 'his' council, it is only to be expected that the semi-literate ex-peasants who make up so high a percentage of the Polish and Yugoslav work forces would not bother much about theirs.

In conclusion, we have seen that the works councils set up in Europe do frequently exercise their prerogatives and are often sensitive to the desires of their workers but that the latter themselves pay little attention to the councils. This would seem to augur badly for those who wish similar councils set up in a participatory democracy to give men control over their lives while at work; but we can draw no conclusions whatsoever as to the general effect of participatory democracy on the development of a self-governing citizenry until we have some attention to the activities of certain other bodies whose creation the participatory democrat would advocate.

FOOTNOTES TO CHAPTER V

1. Jacobs and Landau, *The New Radicals,* p. 154.
2. *Ibid.,* p. 160.
3. *Ibid.,* p. 155.
4. These paragraphs on the German law relating to works councils are taken from Klein, Alfons, *Mitbestimmung-Betriebsverfassung-Personalvertretung* (Stuttgart: M. Kohlhammer Verlag, 1962), pp. 26-37.
5. Dragnich, Alex, *Tito's Promised Land* (New Brunswick: Rutgers University Press, 1954), pp. 184-187.
6. Kolaja, Jiri, "A Yugoslav Workers' Council" *Human Organization,* 20:27, Spring, 1961.
7. See Joint Translation Service, *Summary of the Yugoslav Press,* February 17, 1963, p. 26.
8. *Ibid.,* January 5, 1962, p. 4.
9. Loucks, W. N., "Workers' Self-Government in Yugoslav Industry," *World Politics,* 11:68, October, 1958.
10. Neal, Fred W., *Titoism in Action* (Berkeley; California University Press, 1958), p. 139. Josip Obradovic, John French, Jr., and Willard L. Rodgers conclude that blue collar works council members have less influence than their counterparts from the ranks of management. See their articles "Workers' Councils in Yugoslavia," *Human Relations,* Oct., 1970, vol. 23, p. 459, 470.
11. Wagner, Hardy R. H., *Erfahrungen mit dem Betriebsverfassungsgesetz,* (Köln: Bund-Verlag GMBH, 1960), pp. 82-90.
12. *Ibid.,* p. 95.
13. *Ibid.,* pp. 91-94.
14. *Ibid.,* p. 88.
15. Sturmthal, Adolph, *Workers' Councils* (Cambridge: Harvard University Press, 1964) pp. 76-81. A recent article mentions that the German works councils have had in practice "considerable influence in setting wages and working conditions." See Bussey, Ellen, "Management and Labor in West Germany," *Monthly Labor Review,* August 1970, p. 28, 31.

16. Neal, *op. cit.*, pp. 141-142.
17. Universite Libre de Bruxelles-Institut de Sociologie Solvay-Centre d'Étude des Pays de l'est (ed.), *Le Régime et Les Insti tutions de la République Fédérative* de Yugoslavie (Brussels: Universite Libre de Bruxelles, 1959), p. 68.
18. Singleton & Topham, Yugoslav Workers' Councils — The Latest Phase, *New Left Review,* Jan.-Feb. 1963, p. 80.
19. "Yugoslavia Orders Control of Prices," *New York Times,* Apr. 25, 1962, p. 7.
20. See, e.g., Neuloh, Otto, *Der Neue Betriebsstil* (Tübingen: B. Mohr, 1960), pp. 175-76; Potthoff, Blume and Duvernell, *Zwischenbilanz der Mitbestimmung* (Tubingen: J. C. B. Mohr (Paul Siebeck), 1962), pp. 228-32.
21. "German Union Apathy for Works Councils," *The Times* (London) Jan. 3, 1963, p. 16.
22. Spiro, H. J., *The Politics of German Codetermination,* (Cambridge: Harvard University Press, 1958) p. 92, 135.
23. Neal, *op. cit.,* p. 142.
24. Kolaja, Jiri, *A Polish Factory* (Lexington, Ky.: University of Kentucky Press, 1960), p. 139.

VI

PARTICIPATORY DEMOCRACY
IN MODERN AMERICA

America, like every other major nation, has been subjected to strong centripetal forces ever since the turn of the twentieth century. We have noted this tendency in our first chapter; let us add here that this upsurge in the functions and power of the national government has been accompanied by a continued concentration in industry and that this phenomenon of centralization in both the political and economic spheres shows no signs of vanishing. There are, however, "pockets" of American life where an attempt is made to give some or all of those affected by the policy of certain institutions some say as individuals in determining the rules which constitute this policy. Most of these "recesses" are at the opposite ends of the rainbow: the university and the urban slum. The faculty of an American college or university almost always has the right to play an important role in the operation of its institution; while, for example, the Economic Opportunity Act of 1964 gave the slum poor the authority to participate in developing the War on Poverty programs which would lift their neighborhoods out of their rut. And it will be the purpose of this chapter to consider whether the average faculty member is indeed self-governing in his working life and whether the average inhabitant of the neighborhoods touched by the war on poverty and similar legislation is in fact politically self-governing with respect to the "battles" waged in his neighborhood. These results will then be "checked" by looking very briefly at a recent experiment with participatory democracy that covers every neighborhood of one large American city. (The data in this and the previous chapter will, of course, help us learn whether the small scale institutions of a participatory democracy would in fact make men self-governing.)

Our analysis of academe will be based upon two things: my own experience over the past several years as a junior member of the faculties of two colleges and a recent study of faculty involvement in decision-making sponsored by the American Council on Education.[1] The formal devices by which the faculty can exercise control over university policy-making are several, though, of course, not all exist at every university. There is the Departmental meeting, at which all the members of the discipline in question get together and resolve certain issues. There is the meeting of the entire faculty, common enough at the smaller schools, but a rarity at the larger university. Some colleges have a faculty council, a body elected by the faculty from among its own members which has the right to determine those issues which in the smaller institutions the faculty as a whole has the authority to resolve. Many have a university senate, whose prerogatives vary widely from school to school. And every such institution has a wide range of departmental and faculty committees, some of which are *ad hoc* but most of which specialize in a given area of policy, e.g., curriculum, admissions, etc. (It is true that in recent years students have been given the right in some colleges to participate on faculty committees, but it is still too soon to determine whether or not this experiment will succeed. A student government elected by the student body is, of course, almost universal, but we can exclude it from our study because its powers are usually rather trivial, a truth recognized most clearly by the students themselves.)

It should be noted that some of these devices for insuring faculty control over the university are based on the theory of "direct democracy." That is, policy-making organs such as the departmental meeting and the college-wide faculty meeting are not composed of persons elected by those who will be subject to the policy they promulgate but are, rather, the entire body of those men and women. Now we said in Chapter III, when discussing what individuals could be considered politically self-governing, that any member of a representative legislature which is not simply a rubber stamp for a party boss or dictator deserves this appellation, for even the most timid or corrupt legislator of this sort will at times be influenced by his own ideology when voting on a bill. Though the departmental and faculty meetings are not representative legislatures, nonetheless for the following reasons every "member" of these particular direct democracies is, by virtue of that very fact, self-governing with respect to the policy that affects his working life. Even the most junior and quietest department member sometimes says something that will change the minds of one or more of his fellow professors. In addition, closed votes on disputed issues are by no means unknown, which means, of course, that each person present at the meeting sometimes has the "deciding vote;" and this is even true for some meetings of the entire faculty. Likewise, when one casts a ballot at both these types of sessions, he usually does not pay overly much attention to the wishes of the departmental chairman but, rather, acts in accordance with his own view of what is most desirable under the circumstances. Nor does the department or faculty always blindly accept the recommendations of its committees or of the administration. The author of this book remembers, for example, leading a successful fight against an administration proposal to have faculty advisers write a letter evaluating each of their advisees. (These letters would have involved a lot of paperwork which was, moreover, unnecessary because a student will usually get three letters of reference from professors who know him. In addition, it is difficult to evaluate the performance of an advisee whom one has never had in class.) And at another faculty meeting a committee proposal that the college be permitted "on the odd occasion" to accept funds for secret research was defeated under urging by certain faculty members who contended that research under university auspices ought never to be secret.

But this conclusion that the faculty of an American university is self-governing in its working life needs to be hedged about with several extremely important qualifications. (The broader significance of the conclusion and its qualifications and the other findings on academic self-governance will be discussed at the beginning of the next chapter.) In the first place, as we noted in our discussion of who is politically self-governing, some individuals are usually more so than others. To apply this idea in the context with which we are now concerned, some faculty members have a good deal more to say about the framing of university policy than do others. In the departmental and faculty meetings, a few, either because of their prestige, seniority, position, or eloquence can sway a good number of votes while some have a hard time convincing anybody besides themselves, and others remain completely silent. Moreover, the reports and decisions of committees *are* often accepted without much discussion. In addition, the rules which the faculty as a whole or the departmental meeting are called upon to decide are often trivial, involving, e.g., how many courses a student with two incompletes the previous semester will be permitted to take, whether a course in American History must be taken by all history majors, etc. More fundamental questions, such as whether students should have to major at all, whether the college should offer education and/or business courses, how much the college will be permitted to spend during the forthcoming academic year, how this budget should be allocated among the various departments, who will be given tenure, etc. are often not decided either by the departmental meeting or by the faculty as a whole and this means, in turn, that the average faculty member as an individual is in no sense self-governing with respect to them.

The above-mentioned American Council on Education study of faculty participation in decision making supports some of the conclusions reached above on the basis of personal experience. The author, Archie Dykes, does not employ the definition of "self-governing" individual that we have been using throughout this book and thus does not specifically ask whether the various devices for faculty participation we have noted have in fact made the average faculty member a "self-governing individual" in this sense. And yet the answers his respondents gave to the queries he posed are relevant for our purposes. The departmental meetings were perceived as the institution on campus that was by far and away the most successful in giving faculty members some real decision-making power,[2] which is evidence in turn, that the personal views of the average professor to some extent influence the regulations formulated here. As Dykes says, describing the reaction of the faculty to the question of whether or not the departmental meeting provided an opportunity for meaningful participation in setting policy, "The personal, face-to-face relations . . . between faculty members and administrators at this level . . . contribute to a sense of personal involvement in decision-making that is lacking at other levels of participation."[3] Moreover, further evidence that the views of a substantial number of faculty members count, albeit to a very limited degree, in drafting college policy is seen by the responses to the question of whether the faculty was sufficiently involved in decision-making. Two percent answered "yes;" forty-four percent thought that the situation was not ideal, but that it was just about what one could realistically expect; and fifty-one percent thought that the faculty was too little involved.[4] If none of the institutions of faculty control were functioning so as to give the individual faculty member some real power, the percentage checking the last-mentioned answer probably would have been much higher. On the other hand, were these institutions operating so as to afford him a great deal such power, it is likely that answer #1 would have been the preferred choice of more than two percent.

In the light of the fact that ninety-six percent of those who answered the above question evidently thought the faculty should be given *more* control over university policy, one might think that it would eagerly take advantage of every opportunity offered it to participate in the governance of the school. Such an assumption would be especially justified because, unlike the average factory worker, the usual college professor is neither afraid to speak up nor of the opinion that some aspects of the policy of his institution are beyond his understanding. But the survey showed that *only fifteen percent* of those eligible to participate in the university senate regularly attended its meetings.[5] And the author comes to the general conclusion that there exists "a pervasive ambivalence in faculty attitudes toward participation in decision-making. The faculty members interviewed overwhelmingly indicated the faculty should have a strong, active, and influential role in decisions, especially in those areas directly related to the educational function of the university. At the same time, the respondents revealed a strong reluctance to give the time such a role would require. Asserting that faculty participation is essential, they placed participation at the bottom of their professional priority list and deprecated their colleagues who did participate."[6]

In fact, there were even some areas of concern to the university with respect to which the faculty did not want to have decision-making power. While eighty-six percent of the faculty felt it should control academic affairs (e.g., curriculum, degree requirements) and sixty-nine percent felt that its word should govern in personnel matters such as appointment, promotion and tenure; eighty-one percent and seventy-five percent respectively wished to afford it advisory power only in the areas of financial affairs (e.g., allocation of the budget) and capital improvements (e.g., construction of new buildings).[7] And yet it takes only a little bit of thought to see that the way in which the budget is divided up and decisions about which departments shall have the new laboratories and classrooms will have at least as much effect on one's working life as a determination that, e.g., majors in political science will have to take twenty-four credits in this discipline. One more instance of faculty interest or lack of such in self-governance can be described here. A few years ago, in a well-publicized episode, black students barricaded the gates to the gates to the campus of the City College of New York to demand the admission of more blacks and Puerto Ricans to the school. Dr. Buell Gallagher, the then president of the College, decided it should remain closed during the negotiations with the dissidents. He asked that the tenured faculty, numbering about six hundred, back his decision. Though the issue posed by his request was a crucial one, for no academic institution can function well if it too frequently gives in to expressed or implied threats of force, a total of two hundred and fifty seven (i.e., less than fifty percent) of the tenured faculty turned up for the vote, which initially went against Gallagher one hundred and thirty-six to one hundred and twenty-one. Because of some confusion about procedure, the President succeeded in continuing the meeting until 5 p.m. By that time, only ninety-seven of the tenured faculty were left and these persons upheld his action eight-two to fifteen. Thus more than fifty percent of the tenured C.C.N.Y. faculty demonstrated that they did not care whether the school would surrender to threats of violence while an additional thirty-five percent showed that they were more interested in eating dinner than in resolving the question![8]

In the euphoric pre-Vietnam days of the administration of President Lyndon B. Johnson, the Economic Opportunity Act of 1964 was viewed as the key to the elimination of poverty in America within a few years. When the measure was passed, it was divided into two major Titles. Title I involved nothing new under the sun: the Job Corps and Neighborhood

Youth Corps which it authorized were but carbon copies of various New Deal measures designed to reduce job unemployment, especially among poor youth. Title II, Part A of the Act, however, envisaged the use of "community action" programs to put an end to poverty. These programs have included pre-kindergarten classes to give disadvantaged three to five year olds familiarity with concepts, words, and usages of words that most of them do not meet at home (the well-known "Operation Head Start"); tutoring sessions for school children who have fallen behind their classmates; a Legal Services Program which has given perhaps a million poor people free legal advice; classes for the mentally retarded; employment centers and manpower training courses; child care advice; neighborhood health centers, etc. Debate has raged loud and long about the value of these community action programs — many say, for example, that the advantage obtained through Headstart disappears within a year or two of the child's first exposure to the public school system, while defenders of the programs contend that Headstart plus special classes later will work wonders; that the Legal Services program has made the poor more able to defend themselves against unscrupulous landlords, welfare workers, public housing projects directors, and sellers; and that the neighborhood health centers will radically improve the health of the nation's poor once Congress becomes more generous with its funding. But it is not our job here to discuss the wisdom or lack of such of these various approaches; rather, it is to see what has happened in the application of that section of Title II of the Act which determines how they are to be formulated and administered.

The relevant words are these: A community action program must be "developed, conducted and administered with the maximum feasible participation of residents of the areas and members of the groups served." Legislative history on the meaning of these words was almost non-existent; but the Office of Economic Opportunity soon developed a rule of thumb that each of the "community action agencies," i.e., the bodies responsible for the formulation and implementation of the "community action programs," must have at least one-third of its membership drawn from the ranks of the poor or the areas which the programs would benefit.[9] (The other members of these agencies would represent the city, labor unions, churches, businesses, and social work agencies in the affected neighborhoods. The one-third requirement developed by the OEO was soon written into the Act itself.) So the community action programs of the War Against Poverty begin to meet the demands of those who call for the establishment of a participatory democracy; they give those who will be affected by a course of action some right to determine what that course will be and how it will be administered. What we want to study here is whether the poor exercise this prerogative in practice (especially with respect to projects emanating from neighborhood-wide community action agencies).

Let us now ascertain the percentage of persons eligible to vote in elections for representatives to community action agencies who actually cast a ballot. If the percentage is very small, we have very strong evidence that most of the people affected by the various community action programs are not in fact participating in the development or administration of these activities, and that therefore the creation of these agencies has not made them politically self-governing. Of course, it may be that a good number of those who do not bother with the election still attempt to convince one of the members of the agency to side with them on issues which crop up in the creation or implementation of the program, but this is rather unlikely. If John Jones, slum resident, did not go to the polls to choose a member of the local poverty board, the chances are that for one reason or another he will not attempt to make his views on, e.g., its Headstart program known to those who sit on it.

The turnout at the community action board elections has

been disappointing, so disappointing in fact that the OEO appointed the American Arbitration Association to make a study to discover what went wrong with the earliest set. In the words of a writer who studied that report plus some Congressional hearings:

"Prior to passage of the amendment requiring one-third of the membership of community action agencies to be composed of representatives of the poor, OEO held several elections to select representatives of the poor to take part in running community action programs. They were costly failures.

In the Watts area of Los Angeles, OEO set up 154 polling places, chartered 25 buses to take people to the polls, paid for the printing of 100,000 leaflets and ran up total expenses of $61,000. (In addition, 600 volunteers rang doorbells to get out the vote.) Of the 400,000 considered eligible to vote, only 2,659 did so. That came to less than 1%, at a cost of $22.94 a vote.

In Boston 2.4 voted at a cost per vote of $10.58. In Cleveland a 4.2% turnout cost $1.07 a vote. In Kansas City, a 5% turnout cost $1.89 a vote."[10]

One could contend that these particular statistics are not directly relevant for our purposes, for they involved elections in big cities for *city-wide* rather than *neighborhood* anti-poverty boards. However, there is no reason to believe that, other things being equal, the turnout for a neighborhood poverty board election would be much higher. Secondly, and more importantly, the factors that were discovered to have reduced interest here could, as we shall see later, affect any sort of neighborhood elections. It is for these reasons that even these extensive contests are of interest to us.

There is also available a considerable amount of data concerning the turnout in *neighborhood* poverty board elections and in elections for poverty boards in small towns which are not much bigger than city neighborhoods; and, on the whole, the interest manifested in these polls was hardly overwhelm-

ing either. In Huntsville, Alabama, the turnout was 15.6%
while in Chester, Pennsylvania, the figure was 6%.[11] In Philadelphia, each of twelve poverty areas elected a twelve-mem-
ber Community Action Committee. No one under twenty-one
could vote, but anyone living in the relevant neighborhoods
who was this age or older could go to the polls irrespective
of whether or not he personally was "poor." The total number throughout the city who voted totalled only 13,500, which
was only 3.75% of what the citywide anti-poverty committee
estimated to be a total "potential vote" of 360,000. It is true
that this figure was almost ten percent of the 140,000 or so
poor citizens eligible to vote in these neighborhoods, but it
amounted to only 1.62% of the total number of people of
voting age who happened to live there.[12]

In the Western Addition neighborhood in San Francisco,
with about 62,000 people, only several thousand helped pick
an area board. Moreover, this election was not a one-day af-
fair, but lasted over a period of four or five months.[13] In the
Mission district of the same city, with a total population of
140,000 of whom about 35,000 were considered poor, less
than 600 persons voted in the elections for a board for that
area.[14] In Santa Clara, California, County elections for members of the poverty boards for the "poverty areas" in the
county (as well as for the members of the county-wide Economic Opportunity Committee itself) " . . . in numerous
cases had to be rescheduled owing to the small number of
voters. In retrospect, the elections appear to have been expensive and time-consuming and to have produced much
less participation than expected. In one area, for example, a
board member charged that the election cost $42 per vote
cast."[15] In three "target" communities in Oakland, California,
only two hundred votes were cast in each of the elections for
the members of "target area" committees."[16] Staying in California, it is only fair to note, however, that in contests to
select a board in the Hunters Point area of San Francisco,
where about one-third of the people at the time of the ballot-

ing lived in public housing units, at least one person from 85% of these units voted.[17]

In New York City over twenty-five areas have been designated as "poverty areas." There is a city-wide poverty agency, but, more importantly for our purposes, there exists an agency called a "community corporation" in each of these areas (e.g., Lower East Side, Central Harlem, Bedford-Stuyvesant, Williamsburg, South Bronx) whose purpose it is to plan and coordinate poverty programs at the local level. For example, the local board that recommends poverty programs for the neighborhoods on Staten Island which have been grouped together in one poverty area is called the "Staten Island Community Corporation." During late 1968 and early 1969, elections were conducted for positions on the governing boards of these corporations. As we said previously, federal (and city) law require that at least one-third of the membership on these boards be selected in this way; but in some cases a majority owe their seats to neighborhood elections. Thus the Staten Island Community Corporation as originally constituted contained thirty-two elected directors, who in turn appointed an additional sixteen persons from Island neighborhoods outside the poverty zones. Voting requirements differ slightly from area to area; but in general anyone, rich, middle class, or poor, who is eighteen or over and who has resided in the neighborhood for more than six months is eligible to vote.

The Community Development Agency of the Human Resources Administration of New York City made a valiant effort to insure a large turnout at each of these elections. They were announced in the local press and on posters attached to telephone poles and put in store windows; figures of importance in the areas were asked to spread the word about the forthcoming balloting; and the candidates held public meetings at which they explained their positions. On Staten Island, moreover, the Staten Island Planning Committee, which supervised the election for its successor the Staten Island Community Corporation, used sound trucks, door-to-door canvassing, and buttons to publicize the contest. It eliminated the "long ballot" problem by allotting the thirty-two positions among the six poverty pockets that made up the Staten Island poverty area and having the voters in each of these subdivisions vote only for the positions given to their area. For example, one of the poverty pockets is New Brighton, located near the terminus of the Staten Island ferry. Of the thirty-two vacancies, New Brighton's share was seven, which meant in turn that a citizen of that neighborhood could pick seven names from a list of twenty-three, all of whom were New Brighton residents, and was not faced with the horrifying prospect of choosing thirty-two men and women from a roll of eighty.

Notwithstanding the use of these various devices to get voters to the polls, the turnout in the elections was a great disappointment to the officials of the Community Development Agency who were responsible for their conduct and who, together with the local planning commissions, worked long and hard in planning and administering them. On the average, for example, ten percent of what the Community Development Agency calls the "target population" in six of these neighborhoods — Bushwick in Brooklyn, Coney Island in Brooklyn, the Middle-West Side in Manhattan, Tremont in the Bronx, the Staten Island Poverty Area, and the Upper West Side in Manhattan — voted in these community corporation contests, which an official of the CDA to whom I spoke termed a "low figure". (The target population of a poverty area is apparently its poor and non-white population eligible to vote. In many poverty areas, the "target population" may be close to the total number of those eligible to vote. However, the poverty area designation the "Mid-West Side" includes the middle-class apartment buildings on Central Park West, Riverside Drive, and West End Avenue as well as some horrible tenements, and thus a considerable percentage of its eligible-to-vote residents is not included in its "target population.")

To get a bit more specific, the total number of people eligible to vote in the six communities that in 1968-69 comprised Staten Island's poverty area was estimated by the Staten Island Planning Commission at something like 25,000. However, only 1,374 persons bothered to participate in the voting for the elective members of the Staten Island Community Corporation, which amounts to a five and one half percent participation rate. And the Commission estimated the turnout in one of the six "pockets," the New Brighton area, at about fifteen percent, which means that the figure for some of the other communities was less than 5 percent. In sum, New York's initial experience with anti-poverty elections produced more voter interest than did OEO's try in, e.g., Watts; but we are nonetheless forced to conclude that it induced few of New York's poor to help develop the programs that will, hopefully, write *finis* to the misery under which they live. Nor is there anything in subsequent community corporation contests to cause us to alter this conclusion. Only about 5% of the eligibles participated in the fifteen elections held in the city during September, 1970. To turn again to the Staten Island poverty areas for a more detailed example, five communities, with a total population of perhaps fifteen to twenty thousand, were this time considered part of this area. Only 600 residents, certainly less than 5% of those who could have done so, cast ballots in this particular contest![18]

To continue this discussion of the extent to which the residents of American slums control the War on Poverty boards in their several neighborhoods, we should mention a recently published book whose purpose is to defend the thesis that city neighborhoods should be transformed into political units and given many — though not all — of the powers now exercised by the city government. Milton Kotler's *Neighborhood Government*[19] is a study springing out of his experiences working for the East Central Citizens Organization of Columbus, Ohio (which he refers to as ECCO). This organization did not begin as an agency which was supposed to administer Title II of the Economic Opportunity Act in its community, East Central Columbus — a neighborhood which Kotler describes as covering:

"approximately one square mile, with 6500 residents. It is an area close to the central business district of the city.

Except for a small number of white residents from Appalachia, the people of ECCO are predominantly black. It is a poor community, with an unemployment rate of . . . 25% before ECCO began, compared with a city-wide level of 2%. Even presently it is estimated that 25% of the residents are on welfare. By all statistical criteria, it is what we now call a poverty area."[20]

It started, rather, as a non-profit corporation set up to take control of a settlement house which had formerly been operated by a Lutheran Church. However, at the time Kotler was writing his book, ECCO was relying on the U.S. Office of Economic Opportunity to meet most of its annual budget of about $200,000. It carries on a wide range of programs designed to help the area, including job training, recreational activities, day care of children, health services, and purchasing homes for rehabilitation.

The constitution of ECCO is described by Kotler as democratic. In his words:

"Under the by-laws . . . any resident at least sixteen years old who lives within the boundaries of the corporate territory can . . . become a member. The fundamental authority of the corporation is derived from its membership, which meets in assembly to elect the council members and chairman, and to transact legislative business over the laws, programs and budget of ECCO. Its assemblies require a quorum of 10 percent of the members; they have been legally convened nine times in the past three years. The Executive Council now has thirty members, elected both from . . . four neighborhood clubs . . . and at large in an annual assembly . . . The council has executive authority, and legislative power is vested in the assembly."[21]

In other words, ECCO, like the college department and faculty meeting, is a version of the direct democracy of the New England town meeting, and all the citizens of the community who complete the formality of joining the corporation — which is accomplished simply by signing one's name to a roster — are eligible to vote in the legislature which is supposed to control this neighborhood political system.

Despite these liberal roles which make it easy for everyone in East Central Columbus to have some say as an individual in molding its "government's" policy, the great majority of the inhabitants of this district do not make their voices heard for this purpose. According to Kotler, attendance at the gatherings of ECCO's legislature — i.e., of the neighborhood residents who belong to ECCO — "generally runs between 10 and 25 percent of the membership."[22] There is no indication of how many eligible residents of the area are members, but even assuming that this figure is almost 100%, all we can say is that a maximum of 10 to 25% of those who could have some say as individuals in operating this organization in fact have such a voice.

Kotler insists that he is not worried by this low level of attendance. He points out that in some "regular" political elections in the United States, the turnout is less than 25%. Likewise a turnout of 10 to 25% *is* enough to make sure that all the views and interests which have some support in the neighborhood will be represented at the legislative session.[23] Persons versed in the field of opinion sampling would agree that all positions held by any significant segment of a community could be represented in a 10 to 20% sample of that group, though they would probably dispute Kotler to the extent that he asserts that in the situation he describes the 20% or so who turned up at the session would *necessarily* be a representative cross section of the community. But this

is by-the-by for our purposes, of course. The point is that we
cannot say that the average inhabitant of East Central Columbus is more active as an individual in shaping the policy
of his neighborhood government than in framing that of the
governments of the city of Columbus, of the state of Ohio,
or of the United State of America. It is true that it is in
theory easier for him to help make the decisions issuing from
ECCO than those proceeding from any of the other polities
mentioned. He is probably one of 50,000 or so constituents
of his state senator; while if he is relatively articulate he can
get up in ECCO's assembly, convince several of his fellows
of the rightness of his views on a certain measure, and perhaps as a result defeat or push through that bill — though
under our definitions he would have to be called politically
self-governing even if the condition mentioned in the last
clause were not met. But his failure even to show his face
at the meeting of the ECCO legislature prevents him from
taking part as an individual in developing its policy as effectively as the large size of legislative districts keeps him
from playing such a role in the development of the policy
of the state of Ohio. (It is true that Kotler, unlike most anti-
bureaucratic radicals, does not seem to consider the development of a politically self-governing citizenry as a major reason
for the creation of institutions such as the neighborhood government; but what we have said is valid nonetheless.)

Another factor in addition to the low turnout in board
elections, etc., that makes it impossible for us to claim that
the neighborhood anti-poverty boards have done much in
the way of making the poor in the affected areas self-governing, is that the members of these agencies who have been selected by the poor sometimes let themselves be dominated by
middle-class selectees. As Ralph Kramer says about one of
the poverty areas into which Santa Clara, California, county
had been divided: "In Area 8 the elected representatives of
the poor, all of whom were themselves poor, usually failed
to attend the board meetings. When present, most of them

were silent, intimidated by the other directors. . . . "[24] And a recent book by Kenneth B. Clark and Jeannette Hopkins notes the "passivity among many who, when chosen to represent the poor, are pleased to be accepted by middle-class leadership and function with docility."[25] In addition, some poor people who have become active in the anti-poverty corporations also hold themselves aloof from their constituents. "Many of the professional anti-poverty organizers have become a new class in the slums, apart from and above the poor, who are supposed to be the beneficiaries of these programs. Some critics have coined the term 'povertycrats' to describe these professionals."[26] When workers elect a council which becomes a tool of management they, as individuals, cannot be said to be in charge of the factory; and when poor people elect a representative to an anti-poverty board who usually does what its more articulate membership tells him to or who ignores their wishes, they, as individuals, cannot be said to be in charge of the program sponsored by the board.

One more federally-aided attempt at bringing "participatory democracy" to slum America should be mentioned here. The Model Cities Program was enacted in 1966 as part of President Johnson's Great Society Program. Because of the Vietnam War, however, it was poorly funded by Congress at first, and is just now starting to have an impact. Under the program, the nation's cities select blighted areas within their borders for "total reform:" i.e., to get money for programs aimed at improving housing, health services transportation, job opportunities, and welfare payments and at reducing crime and juvenile delinquency in these depressed neighborhoods. Though the elected government of the city or county will have the final say as to what will be done in its "model" neighborhoods, the Model Cities Act requires "widespread citizen participation" in the model cities program. New York City has met this requirement by setting up commissions in its three Model Cities neighborhoods, Harlem, East Harlem,

Central Brooklyn, and the South Bronx. These commissions, to be selected by all the adult citizens of the areas, will in practice have a good deal to say about how the model cities money is spent. As of March, 1969, two of the three commissions had been elected. Central Brooklyn, with approximately 400,000 residents, saw only 1,500 lonely souls come out to vote for its board. The South Bronx was somewhat more successful: 4,000 out of 315,000 inhabitants participated in the balloting; and this figure, though small, was better than that recorded in the area on primary election days. Then, in spring of 1971, the city government ordered new Model Cities elections in these three neighborhoods. (At present, the commision is called a "policy committee" and all residents of the areas who are 16 or older are eligible to vote.) The election drew a total of 5000 voters from the neighborhoods: at best about 1% of the eligible voters. On the whole, the results of these model cities elections indicate that the people of the slums in which they were held will be as little involved in the formulation of Model Cities policy as they are in conducting the related (and at least up to now) OEO-administered War on Poverty.[27]

Finally, New York State, in response to certain events which we shall chronicle in subsequent chapters, passed in 1969 a school decentralization law for New York City. This act divided the City into approximately thirty school districts each of which was to be headed by a Community School Board elected by the residents of the district according to a complicated system of proportional representation. These local boards have real though limited powers over curriculum, textbooks, and hiring and firing of school personnel, though the law is very ambiguous about their relationship to the city-wide Board of Education. Once again on the assumption that one who does not vote for the members of an institution will not control them, we have to say that this school decentralization law has not yet sparked the residents of the thirty school districts to set educational policy for their respective areas. The initial school board elections, held in the four "outer" boroughs in March of 1970 and in Manhattan in May of that year, were widely publicized by the city-wide and local press and by city and local groups with an interest in education. On Staten Island, for example, the *Staten Island Advance* published the names, pictures and educational philosophies of all the candidates and endorsed its own slate; a citizen group interested in public education held a candidates' fair at which the voters could speak personally to all the candidates; each candidate was invited to speak at an open meeting held at one of the borough's high schools; and many parish priests urged their congregations to vote for candidates who favored state aid to parochial education. But only 15% of the eligible voters came to the polls in the March contests, and the comparable figure for Manhattan was 9%. Staten Island's turnout was 18.2%; while Brooklyn's District N, including the Ocean-Hill-Brownsville area which provided much of the impetus for the decentralization bill, had a turnout of 4.8%.[28]

To summarize very briefly the findings of this chapter, we have seen that the institutions of the departmental and faculty meeting in colleges and universities do give the faculty member some say as an individual in shaping the rules that govern his working life. He has a real opportunity, especially in the department meeting, to play some part in determining this policy, and most faculty members take at least some advantage of this opportunity. Even in academia, however, many of the important decisions, theoretically the prerogatives of the faculty, are made by committees or by the administration; and most professors show themselves uninterested in being given the right to make budgetary decisions. (Recall here, too, the 1969 New York City College incident, described earlier.) Attempts to involve the slum poor in America in the writing and administration of programs designed to help their neighborhoods have not yet made them politically self-governing. Under two federal laws, the Economic Opportunity Act and the Model Cities Bill, the residents of such neighborhoods are to elect boards with some power to develop such courses of action. However, it is highly unlikely that the average inhabitant of these areas even tries to convince his representative on these boards to implement a particular project he thinks would help the community; the extremely low turnout in the elections to fill the positions in these poverty, etc. boards is ample evidence for this. The experience with the initial all-city local school board elections in New York is fully congruent with all the other results we have set forth above; and that experience is a particularly good "check" on those results since it involved not only very rich, very educated and very poor communities, but also neighborhoods inhabited by blue collar and clerical workers and/or the "middle-middle" class.

FOOTNOTES TO CHAPTER VI

1. This study, by Archie Dykes, is entitled "Faculty Participation in Academic Decision Making" (Washington: American Council on Education, 1968).

2. Dykes, *op. cit.,* p. 30.

3. *Ibid.,* p. 30.

4. *Ibid.,* p. 12.

5. *Ibid.,* p. 31.

6. *Ibid.,* p. 38.

7. *Ibid.,* p. 2.

8. See *New York Times,* April 29, 1969, p. 30.

9. See Donovan, John, *The Politics of Poverty* (New York: Pegasus, 1967) p. 55.

10. Scheibla, Shirley, *Poverty is Where the Money Is* (New Rochelle, N.Y.: Arlington House, 1968), p. 128. The American Arbitration Association Report, published in 1966 in the New York by the American Arbitration Association, is entitled *Representation Elections and Voter Participation in Community Action Programs Under OEO.*

11. "Where were the Poor on Election Day?," *U.S. News & World Report,* March 21, 1966, p. 94.

12. See *New York Times,* November 6, 1965, p. 26.

108   *Participatory Democracy*

13. Kramer, Ralph M., *Participation of the Poor* (Englewood Cliffs, N.J., Prentice Hall, 1969), pp. 37-38.
14. *Ibid.,* pp. 41-42.
15. *Ibid.,* p. 86.
16. *Ibid.,* p. 144.
17. *Ibid.,* pp. 49-51.
18. The information in the above paragraphs on New York City's community corporation elections was obtained from the *Staten Island Advance,* January 29, 1969, p. 6, January 30, 1969, p. 7, and Sept. 30, 1970, p. 2; the *New York Times,* Sept. 20, 1970, p. 43; and personal interviews with some officials at the Community Development Agency of New York City's Human Resources Administration and of the Staten Island Planning Commission.
19. Kotler, Milton, *Neighborhood Government* (Indianapolis: Bobbs-Merrill, 1969).
20. *Ibid.,* p. 44.
21. *Ibid.,* p. 46.
22. *Ibid.,* p. 83.
23. *Ibid.,* p. 83.
24. *Op. cit.,* p. 101.
25. Clark, Kenneth B. and Hopkins, Jeannette, *A Relevant War Against Poverty,* (New York: Harper and Row, 1969), p. 246.
26. *New York Times,* March 29, 1971, p. 26.
27. he information in this paragraph is based upon personal interviews with some officials of the Model Cities Committee of the Office of the Mayor of New York City, and New York *Times* March 29, 1971, p. 20, May 22, 1971 p. 25 and June 12, 1971, p. 15.
28. See the *New York Times,* March 21, 1970, p. 30; March 28, 1970, p. 20 and June 3, 1970, p. 53.

VII

IMPEDIMENTS TO THE SUCCESS
OF PARTICIPATORY DEMOCRACY

The past two chapters should have given the members of the several anti-bureaucratic radical movements some cause for concern. These persons have called for the creation of small-scale and responsive institutions to take over many of the functions of the nation, state, city, centrally and/or privately managed economic or educational units in the hope that the individuals affected by the policy of these institutions will participate as individuals in its formulation. And yet, where these small-scale institutions do exist, this ideal is rarely attained. Some factory workers councils are controlled by one person or a few; some do not exercise their powers; some do, but ignore the wishes of their constituents; and their constituents often take little or no notice of them. The vast majority of the residents of America's urban slum neighborhoods do not even bother to turn out to elect the members of the neighborhood agencies which are to help develop and administer anti-poverty and similar programs. The only such institution whose practice remotely resembles the theory of how participatory democracy would work is the faculty or departmental meeting at a college or university; and it should be noted that this is a "direct democracy" with a well-educated, middle class membership which usually holds its meetings during working hours. Even in the university, attendance at the meetings of the university senate or at important special sessions of the faculty as a whole is often sparse; and most professors want nothing to do with budgetary and similar matters. Thus the institutions we have been observing are light years away from making the average man they serve self-governing politically or vocationally: his views on the issues with which they concern themselves are hardly ever the reasons why at least one member of, e.g., the anti-poverty board for his area or his works council votes the way he does on at least one issue before the board or council.

More important than the fact that ongoing experiments with participatory democracy are failures is the question of *why* they have not worked, i.e., of why they have not in practice led the individuals over whom they have jurisdiction to exercise as individuals some control over the policy they set. (In this chapter, an assertion that an institution is a failure means only that it has not made those to whom it issues rules participants as individuals in framing them — and should not be taken as the equivalent of an assertion that the agency has proven itself totally useless.) If the "why" proves to be a phenomenon that is easily remediable, the anti-bureaucratic radicals have little to worry about, for they can make sure in the future that their reforms are implemented only in situations where this problem has been corrected. However, if it turns out to be a factor or factors which it is difficult to manipulate, the participatory democrats should perhaps begin rethinking their ideas — for then the chances would be high that their ideal society, too, would be plagued by a failure of its numerous small-scale institutions to produce a self-governing citizenry. We must, therefore, turn once again to the various experiences with participatory democracy we have studied, as well as to some ideas formulated by other social scientists, with the intent now of seeing the reasons why the works councils, anti-poverty boards, etc. have not turned out to be organizations whose policy-making the men and women they serve influence as individuals.

To some extent, of course, we have already explained why this is so in our discussion of whether it is so. The elitism of some of these bodies, the dependence non-exercise of their prerogatives by some others, and the apathy of the poor, the workers, and some of the college prfoessors are all in themselves reasons why the institutions of participatory democracy we have considered have not, on the whole, served as a vehicle for "law-giving" by the average man to whom they are responsible. We must discuss these several "causative situations" in a bit more detail, however, to determine just how impossible it is to rid ourselves of them. To do this, in turn, we must look to two general sorts of evidence: (a) are there many cases where the opposite situations prevail? and/or (b) are the social, political, economic and/or psychological conditions from which they themselves spring confined to a few places or relatively easy to eradicate? Thus, for example, if there are a significant minority of cases where the poor take an interest in the doings of their anti-poverty boards and where the factory workers concern themselves with the behavior of their works council, we can assert with some confidence that it will not be too difficult in the future to stimulate widespread curiosity about the actions of institutions of participatory democracy. Likewise, if we discover that the lack of interest in anti-poverty boards that we have found is solely the product of a failure to have neighborhood people run for office, the anti-bureaucratic radicals need not despair about the future of these and similar institutions, for in such case the cause of the apathy can easily be eradicated. On the other hand if, for example, it is deeply ingrained in the nature of most men to pay no attention to what happens outside the confines of their family, friends and immediate work group, the apathy springs from a phenomenon that cannot be rooted out without great difficulty; and the decentralist socialists perhaps then ought to conclude that their ideals contain an element of utopianism.

Turning first to the fact that some works councils did not act independently or exert their rights and thus automatically deprived their constituents of all power to help make factory policy, the advocates of participatory democracy can argue with a good deal of justification that it would be highly unfair to contend that this proves in and of itself that their vision of the good society cannot be realized. For, they could argue, and rightly so, that we have adduced evidence here showing that many German and Yugoslavian works councils do in fact make use of their prerogatives; and would conclude from this that it is quite feasible to insure that most of the "local" bodies which they wish to see created can be induced to carry out their functions. Moreover, they would add that where councils or anti-poverty boards have done nothing or have surrendered their decision-making powers to someone else, this has usually been the result of a condition or event which is not widespread or which can easily be remedied. Thus one obvious reason why some Yugoslav councils (indigent members of anti-poverty boards) merely rubberstamped the decisions of the plant director (middle-class members on the boards) was the feeling of their members (of these poor people) that they were not well educated enough to understand the problems the plant (boards) faced. And it is surely possible to educate a community to the level where its working class can solve many such questions — in some cases, admittedly, with the advice of persons well versed in economics, sociology, accounting and/or engineering. Likewise, some works councils in Yugoslavia did not really exercise their powers simply because they fell under the sway of the Yugoslav Communist Party.[1] But, the decentralist socialist could reason, France, the United States, and Great Britain do not have major political parties of the sort that want to dominate every institution in the community, and, consequently, this unfortunate aspect of the Yugoslav experience with decentralization of social and economic institutions is not likely to crop up in these other nations.

It is true, moreover, that some organs of participatory democracy have been stymied by the machinations of those to whose powers they supposedly succeeded. For example, in

Poland certain council decisions were simply ignored by bureaucrats and plant directors who wished to retain their powers,[2] while our discussion of Yugoslav councils revealed the presence of a plant director to whom the existence of the plant's works council was a mere formality. In Poland some plant directors took hold of the ambiguities in the legislation authorizing the existence of works councils to thwart the ambitions of these bodies. Thus the relevant bit of legislation asserted, in one section, that the works council was to manage the plant, but provided, in another paragraph, that the plant director was to direct the activity of the enterprise. And certain directors used this contradiction to try to frustrate the attempts of some councils to utilize their statutory prerogatives.[3] Likewise the mayors of many American cities, including Mayor Daley of Chicago, Mayor Lee of New Haven, Mayor Yorty of Los Angeles and Mayor Shelley of San Francisco fought bitterly to insure that the city-wide and local anti-poverty agencies in the ghetto neighborhoods could not act independently of city hall: the mayors felt that their political position would be weakened if it were realized that they had no control over filling the jobs created by the program. As a result of this pressure, local public agencies now have to be given a say alongside the representatives of the poor in the development of anti-poverty policy.[4]

However, the participatory democrats could aver, and once again with some justification, that the evidence set forth in the above paragraph is no reason for pessimism. It is hardly surprising that endeavors at decentralizing power will be followed by attempts by those who are shorn of their prerogatives to regain them. It is not at all inevitable, though, that these reactions will succeed. If the legislation is precise enough, the old elite will not be able to point to the wording of the law in order to convince the public of the legitimacy of its claims. Thus, if the words "maximum feasible participation of the poor," etc. in the Economic Opportunity Act had been replaced by a clause providing specifically that two-thirds of the members of every city-wide or neighbor-hood community action agency shall be selected by the residents of that neighborhood, Messrs. Daley, Yorty et al. probably would not have been able to reduce the powers of the local boards. Moreover, the participatory democrats would claim, in a country where there are free elections the people can use their political muscle to replace the recalcitrant plant or public officials by individuals who will be more responsive to the claims of the new institutions. For example, if the poor in Chicago do not like Mayor Daley's attempts to dominate the city's anti-poverty boards, they can combine to replace him with a mayor who is more willing to let others make some of the decisions about the city's problems.

To sum up what we have said so far, we noted at the beginning of this chapter that one reason that works councils, anti-poverty boards, etc. have not produced a situation in which their constituents take part in developing the policy that they promulgate is that they themselves often do not make use of their powers or surrender their independence. Another, we saw, is that some are more interested in their own advancement than in aiding their constituents; while yet a third is that these constituents themselves are uninterested in the activities of the council, etc. (When we say in these chapters that one is "uninterested in," "apathetic toward," "does not bother himself with," etc., the activities of an institution, we do not necessarily mean that he is *subjectively* unconcerned; but merely that he engages in no behavior which would enable an impartial observer to infer that he *is* concerned.) We added, however, that if the opposite of these phenomena of non-exercise of power, elitism, and apathy often prevails and/or these phenomena are the result of conditions which are themselves localized or relatively easy to remedy, we would have some evidence that the small-scale institutions the participatory democrats wish to create would achieve this end of individual self-government. So far we have determined that certain of the conditions which produce non-exercise of power by works councils, etc., are localized (e.g., the control of nations by communist parties) and/or far from impossible to remedy (e.g., the creation of these small-scale institutions by extremely vague legislation).

There is data in the last two chapters, moreover, indicating that many institutions of the sort we are studying do exercise their rights — and do so in a manner which responds to the desires (to the extent expressed) of those who elect them. Furthermore, there were examples in Yugoslavia where the council seemed to place a fence between itself and the work force, but we also noted instances both there and in West Germany where it fought for the material interests of the plant's employees. There is thus some evidence upon which to base a prognosis that were "participatory democracy" to be widely implemented in the west, the representative bodies that would then manage the factories, the schools, the universities, and certain public activities taking place in the neighborhoods would act and, when acting, pay close attention to the wishes of their respective electorates. The *behavior* of many of the community action agencies that have been elected under the aegis of the United States Economic Opportunity Act of 1964 is likewise helpful to the case of the decentralist socialist, even though the turnout for elections to these bodies is not. They have sponsored a wide variety of imaginative programs which certainly are designed to help the slum poor (i.e., their constituencies). Included among these are the famous Headstart program for preschool children, manpower training classes, child care courses, cultural events, etc. It is true that some or all of these avenues might turn out to be dead ends, and it is also true that the higher-up officials in a few of these agencies receive salaries that are much higher than that received by their average constituents; but this does not rebut the proposition that their initiation of activities which are intended to remove the causes and/or the consequences of poverty shows that they work for, and do not isolate themselves from, their

116   *Participatory Democracy*

community. Note, too, could also be taken of an institution of participatory democracy which we have not mentioned yet, but which was much in the news a few years ago and whose doings we shall concern ourselves with more in the next chapter. This is the local board that was elected in 1967, two years before the citywide New York City school decentralization bill was enacted, to run the schools in the Puerto Rican and Negro Ocean-Hill-Brownsville neighborhood in Brooklyn. Regardless of what one might think of the overall conduct of this board, it responded to the wishes of its electorate by trying to improve the area schools through hiring top-notch administrators, principals and teachers. Also, the community school board for the area of New York City where the author lives is performing the tasks that the law has assigned to it and, moreover, trying its utmost to satisfy the people of the rapidly-growing area by getting funds for the construction of desperately-needed new schools and classrooms.

Actually, the general experience with representative bodies in western countries where there are free elections should reassure those who are worried about participatory democracy on the ground that the men who will serve as the representatives on, e.g., the neighborhood boards will ignore their electorates' demands. When the majority of the public is firmly convinced that an issue should be resolved in a particular way, the city council, state legislature, Congress, or Parliament will respond appropriately — sooner or later. It is true that often the vast majority of a legislator's constituents have no feelings whatsoever on a particular issue (e.g., the size of the tariff on bananas) and that in other cases both sides of a question command significant popular support. In these instances, he is more or less free to vote as he wishes — and can in no sense be charged with elitism when he does so. But when the vast majority of the individuals who have chosen him do feel strongly on a particular topic, he will generally vote their way. Nor does the situation that prevails in a body such as the British Parliament where the tradition of party discipline is extremely strong contravene the basic thesis that legislatures freely chosen by the electorate do take into account its wishes. It is true that in Britain an individual MP will usually obey the party whip rather than the wishes of the voters in his constituencies when these conflict occur. But the party leadership will certainly pay attention to popular opinion throughout the country as a whole when deciding what policy to adopt. And, where public opinion does speak "loud and clear," it will respond. Anyone who doubts this is referred to the example of the supposedly egalitarian Labour Party's crackdowns in 1965 and 1968 on colored immigration.

For all the above reasons, the believer in participatory democracy can conclude with a good deal of justification that the elected policy-making bodies which he wishes set up to control places of work and neighborhood services will do their job and, moreover, will do it in accordance with the wishes of the workers, the residents, etc. But we also mentioned a third reason why existing organs of participatory democracy such as works councils and community anti-poverty agencies have not proven devices for getting the average man to influence as an individual the formulation of policy that is of concern to him. This is the simple fact that he is simply not interested in what these organs are doing, and this fact is almost universal concomittant of the presence of these organs. In West Germany, for example, the worker does vote for his representative to the works council but pays no attention to what he does after he takes his seat. And, in the American ghetto, the average man does not even bother to turn out at the election which determines who will represent him on the local anti-poverty agency. Now, unless the causes of this widespread apathy toward works councils, poverty boards, and even university senates are few and limited in scope or easily curable, we will have to conclude that it is likely that the additional organs of participatory democracy which anti-bureaucratic radicals wish to see created will likewise be greeted with widespread indifference — and thus followd by the perpetuation of the *status quo* where the average man has as an individual little or no say in setting the rules which control his behavior. Obviously, if the average citizen does not give a thought to these bodils, he will not as an individual be affecting their determinations! We must, therefore, now turn to a detailed consideration of why existing institutions of participatory democracy have appeared to generate in so many instances little interest on the part of those they are supposed to help and make self-governing. (Note again that when we say in these chapters that one is "apathetic toward," "uninterested in," "does not bother himself with," etc. the activities of an institution, we do not necessarily mean that he is *subjectively* unconcerned; but merely that he engages in no behavior which would enable an impartial observer to infer that he *is* concerned.)

The American Arbitration Association's study of the election of members of anti-poverty boards under the Economic Opportunity Act of 1964 furnishes us with several reasons why these particular contests stirred so little interest, reasons which may also lead to a lack of concern in certain areas of the nation in the functioning of the institutions of a full-fledged participatory democracy. The boards were, after all, to develop and administer a program financed by the national and city governments. And some slum residents viewed this program as simply an attempt to keep the poor man quiet, i.e., as an attempt to bribe him not to riot, rather than as an effort on the part of the American political system to secure meaningful change. What the official at the New York City Human Resources Administration to whom I spoke about the anti-poverty election in that metropolis said essentially confirmed that particular finding. Referring particularly to the causes of the apathy of the residents of the Bedford-Stuyvesant ghetto in Brooklyn to the local anti-poverty agency and program, he noted that they feel that the whole anti-poverty organization is dominated by city employees and politicians. Since they hold that this sort of person is responsible for their present predicament, they will have nothing to do with any activity with which men of this stripe are connected. Their disenchantment with the existing elite has reached such a pass that they are quite unable to believe that anything proceeding from it is really designed for their benefit. Now the defender of participatory democracy could argue, and the argument would have much merit, that this cause of the lack of concern with the activities of the local poverty agencies is a phenomenon that is limited to a few areas. It is true, he would admit, that the transference of power from the nation and state to the city and ward, from the board of directors to the workers, from the central school board to the local school boards, etc., will probably be accomplished by the mechanism of a piece of legislation enacted by the city or state government. However the number of persons whose circumstances are as desperate as those of Bedford-Stuyvesant, and who have received such bad treatment from public officials all their lives is relatively small. This means in turn that most people (and thus most communities) will not respond with cynicism to the establishment of participatory democracy on a widespread basis merely because it was a governmental act which was the formal precondition of the birth of this new type of society. In any case, a government which passed such a bill is likely to be headed by idealistic persons who will not be viewed by even the poor ghetto Negro as "wheeler-dealer" types who are making a minor concession in order to be able to keep power.

Beyond a general suspicion of the present local and national political establishments the American Arbitration Association study listed these more specific and localized causes for the low turnout at the early anti-poverty board elections. In some places, this initial scepticism was enhanced by the fact that the representatives of the poor were to be a minority on the board: a community can hardly be blamed for suspect-

ing that an election is a farce and boycotting it when its results must still leave them in a position of impotence. One
city failed to break down its poor areas into separate election
districts, which meant that the potential voters in a particular
area did not know the first thing about many of the candidates. Even in those municipalities where the election was by
district, many of the men who ran to fill the seats on the
boards had neither charisma nor any sort of reputation. And
some of the attempts to publicize the elections made too much
use of the big newspapers and TV stations and paid little
attention to "local" media of communication such as neighborhood papers, "black-oriented" radio stations, and store-
window placards. Of course, these specific factors reducing
community interest in elections for seats on organs of participatory democracy (and, ultimately, in the activities of these
organs) can be removed with a bit of thought and a willingness to learn from experience. The recent "community corporation" elections in New York City that were described in
the last chapter demonstrate this clearly; for there ample use
was made of posters, publicity in local newspapers, speeches
by influential figures in the neighborhood, and sound trucks.

There is another point made in the Association's study
which may be important for our purpose. It was found that
one reason that there was little thought given to the election
was that there were no genuine disputes among the candidates. Everyone seemed to be agreed that poverty must be
ended and that the poor should have some say in determining how this should be done, but apparently little attempt
was made to discuss specifics which would have led to debate and perhaps to the formation of *ad hoc* political parties
and thus have stimulated interest in the campaign. (As Seymour Lipset has said in another context, a "stable democracy" requires not only consensus but, as well, "the mani-
festation of conflict or cleavage.") [5] But it is quite possible
that though the initial elections for the organs of participatory democracy may be rather dull affairs, as an institution

suggests, enacts and administers programs, opposition is bound to develop. For example, the neighborhood anti-poverty board may decide to emphasize education for pre school children. If the neighborhood contains a great number of people who cannot get a decent job because they are totally unskilled, a demand might arise in some quarters for the board to devote more attention to vocational courses for adults. If it refuses and persists in concentrating on the pre-schoolers, its elective membership may be continually bombarded by requests from various members of the community and be faced with an opposition slate at the next election, a slate which promises to be responsive to these suggestions. Even if few disputes arise over issues, moreover, personality struggles within the board itself or between the board and outsiders may well develop, which should add color to its activities and to the next election.

Thus certain specific factors that have plagued the anti-poverty elections and kept many persons from taking part in them certainly do not have to continue to be a thorn in the side of the anti-poverty agencies and similar institutions; and, moreover, the introduction of participatory democracy on a broad scale will not necessarily be accompanied by the same scepticism that has made people in slum areas reluctant to pay much attention to the anti-poverty agencies. However, we cannot assume that the disappearance or modification of these factors will lead to the development of the popular interest in the workings of works councils, anti-poverty boards, etc., that is a condition of their making men and women self-governing. For example, even the poverty board elections that were held *after* it was decided to publicize them thoroughly drew few voters, as we saw in the last chapter. And a recent anti-poverty board election in Newark featured a bitterly-fought contest between supporters of black playwright Leroi Jones and persons who probably were backed by Mayor Kenneth Gibson. In the campaign charges of racism and corruption were often heard and one would have expected the electorate to turn out in large numbers. But the Jones slate won by 2 to 1 in balloting which saw only 752 out of the 12,000 persons who were qualified to vote come to the polls.[6] So we must continue our search for the reasons why not much interest is shown in existing organs of participatory democracy.

Let us take as a starting point the arena whose "average man" does to some extent in fact participate as an individual in policy-making, i.e., the university. We saw that the department faculty meeting is in fact usually attended by most members of the department, and that most members of the department have at least some hand in contributing to the decisions that emanate from these meetings. We also saw that the faculty studied in the Dykes report says that it wishes to become more involved in certain areas of policy making. On the other hand, only fifteen percent of those who were eligible to attend the meetings of the senate of that university regularly did so — and less than half the tenured faculty of City College of New York turned out for a vote on whether the college should remain closed after some of its students shut it down by actions which carried with them a threat of the use of force in case their demands were resisted. More important is Dykes' conclusion — which we have already quoted but which should be reiterated again — that there exists "a pervasive ambivalence in faculty attitudes toward participation in decision making. The faculty members interviewed overwhelmingly indicated that the faculty should have a strong, active and influential role in decisions, especially in those areas directly related to the educational function of the university. At the same time, the respondents revealed a strong reluctance to give the time such a role would require. Asserting that faculty participation is essential, they placed participation at the bottom of their professional priority list and deprecated their colleagues who did participate."[7]

To anyone who has ever been connected with a university as a faculty member, the above statement rings true indeed, and there is no reason to assume that the lack of faculty willingness to participate in university governance which it describes will change in the near future. Admittedly, the average faculty member will keep on going to the departmental meeting and serve on a committee or two. But the present situation in which he makes little or no attempt to influence members of other committees, the university senate or the administration is likely to continue. The reasons for his avoidance of these chores are obvious, and are set forth explicitly in the Dykes report.[8] First and foremost, when one goes about from person to person and from committee to committee telling them that the university should do this or that he will have little time for his own work. Now, at least in recent years, people have been attracted into university teaching simply because it affords them an opportunity to extend the sum of human knowledge in an area of interest to them. In other words, numerous professors enter academia in order to do research, not in order to spend their time setting the university straight. To the extent they do the latter, they have no time for the former, and few professors think that the game of university politics is worth the loss of time for research. This is especially true when an additional reason for concentrating all one's energies upon scholarship enters onto the scene into the form of the "publish or perish rule," which means, in short, that one will be fired unless he produces a certain respectable quantity of books, monographs, and articles. Admittedly, the publish or perish rule is not in force in all universities in the country, and where it is operative it is applied more ruthlessly in some schools than in others, but it certainly does act as a deterrent to faculty participation in university administration. This may not be good, but it is the case, and is likely to remain so, though perhaps in a slightly diminished degree, for the foreseeable future.

Dykes also notes that some faculty members shun participation in the governing of the university because they fear that to do so will affect their ability as teachers.[9] In other words, many college professors feel it is their duty to be inspiring lecturers as well as good scholars. And to prepare for classes often takes a great deal of time, especially when it is the first time that one has taught the course and the material upon which one bases his lectures is not conveniently compressed into a textbook but is scattered throughout books, articles, newspapers, and what one has come across while doing his own research. It is indubitable for all except the most hardy that spending hours on end urging the university to make certain changes will make it impossible to prepare adequately for one's classes and thus impair one's ability to function at the podium as well as at thee typewriter or in the laboratory. And, in any event, most professors would rather teach than attend committee meetings!

Dykes' findings as to why professors do not as individuals participate more actively in the operation of the university even though they feel they should be doing so are surely applicable, in generalized form, outside the ivory tower. People are busy; and to spend one's time serving on, for example, a local poverty board or pressuring its members takes time which the great majority of men and women just do not have — unless they reduce their participation in other things that are of importance to them. The average man returns home at about 6 p.m.; by the time dinner is finished it is already seven. Assuming that he has children he will certainly want to be with them for the hour or so before their bed. He will then want to read a bit, watch TV, talk to his wife, and before he knows it is time for sleep. Finding out what the poverty board is up to and then paying visits to one or more of its members in order to convert them to his point of view on the need for setting up classes for high school dropouts, will mean not only that he will have to forego these other activities but that he won't have time or energy to visit friends, to go to the theatre or ball game, etc. There are, of course, exceptions to this, especially unmarried men and women who lead relatively solitary lives, but this group makes up only a minority of the adult population.

Another reason why some college teachers refuse to have anything to do with the administration of their school is that the instruments of faculty involvement in its operation often get bogged down in problems that strike many persons as trivial.[10] We noted, for example, that the departmental faculty meeting is often called upon to decide such questions as whether a student who received incompletes in two courses the past semester will be allowed to take a full load during the current term. There are a few departmental politicians who devote much energy and many words to questions such as these, but many professors are so depressed by debating them that they tend to shy away from participation in departmental committees out of a belief that these groups are, or soon will be, debating at length matters of little or no importance.

One can be pretty certain, too, that a good number of the organs of participatory democracy which the anti-bureaucratic left wishes to see created will start busying themselves with concerns which seem to most people rather petty. There is no inherent reason why this situation will be limited to university groups only. As Cook and Morgan note: "Participatory democracy could proliferate decision-making units with essentially parochial concerns, absorbing all attention in the trivial at the expense of what is significant. We may assume that such a situation would quickly erode the citizen's interest and desire to participate actively in such units."[11] For example, an American scholar notes that a Yugoslav workers council spent a good deal of time discussing whether Muslim workers should be allowed time off with pay to repair a mosque.[12] Admittedly this problem is of interest to the particular workers who wish to fix their mosque and simultaneously not lose any of their wages; but it is quite possible that the doings of a council which on the whole concerned itself with issues such as this would soon be ignored by the majority of the plant work force. On the same note, one can visualize an American works council devoting several hours to the problem of whether directional arrows should be painted in the several lanes of the factory's parking lot; an American anti-poverty board behaving similarly on the matter of whether to plant four or five saplings on a ghetto block under the board's neighborhood beautification scheme; and an American neighorhood school board discussing endlessly whether teenage girls ought to be permitted to come to school in slacks. It may be an omen that some of the neighborhood parents who during 1969 involved themselves in studying the problem of school decentralization in New York City ignored crucial questions of curriculum and teacher tenure and agonized over the problem of whether the number of school districts into which the city should be divided should be sixteen, twenty-five, thirty or some other number. This, in turn, discouraged quite a few parents from continuing to participate in these groups. It may be the case that the problems we have mentioned in these two paragraphs are significant; but their objective importance or lack of such is irrelevant for us simply because many of the people to whom the organs of participatory democracy will be responsible will view their consideration as a waste of time.

The Dykes study contends, as we have also previously noted, that a majority of faculty members believe that the faculty ought not to have any decision making power in financial matters.[13] Most professors do not feel that problems of how the money in the hands of the university should be spent or of whether this type of building or that should be constructed are very pertinent to their careers; and yet, for reasons already mentioned, their resolution may in many cases affect one's ability to teach or do research. In any case, one may be certain that most people fail to see the relevance to themselves of matters resolved by particular institutions. Very few people pay any attention to tariff or antitrust legislation even though high tariff and/or concentration in a particular industry may well be the cause of higher consumer prices. And, of course, if one fails to perceive the importance to him of the decisions of a poverty board, a university committee, or the United States Senate he will probably pay little attention to the activities of the institution.

To recapitulate, we have so far analyzed three reasons why many faculty members seem unconcerned about a role in the operation of their university — a lack of time, a belief in the unimportance in what the various organs of faculty self-government discuss, and a failure to see that certain issues are of relevance to them. We have also seen that there is some reason to assume that these three factors will produce a lack of interest in the other organs of participatory democracy favored by the decentralist socialists. Few men and women, whatever their profession, have much spare time beyond that which they devote to necessary rest, family obligations, and a much-desired one or two nights out per week. Small groups outside the university, too, have a tendency to waste their energy upon what seem to most people to be trivialities, and one can predict with a fair amount of confidence that the small groups that will be the policy-making organs in a participatory democracy will also fall into this trap. Finally, most people, outside the university as well as in, cannot visualize how certain problems may affect them and will thus ignore the activities of a "local" board that tries to resolve these matters.

There is an obvious source of the general lack of interest in the activities of the various works concils and poverty boards that we have considered that was not mentioned by any of the studies upon which we have relied but was almost certainly operative. This is the fact that, as many social scientists have indicated, most people are mainly curious about those issues which have some immediate relevance to their personal lives and to those of their families and close friends. "Will my daughter Tessie marry Johnny?" is a question of a lot more importance to most people than is "should the United States expand its public housing program?" "How can my George get out of being drafted?" creates a lot more worry in the minds of his parents than "should the United States be in Vietnam?," even though the main reason that George's folks want to keep him out of the army is the possibility that he will be sent to die in southeast Asia. And, needless to say, "Will my daughter marry Johnny?" and "how can my George avoid the draft?" — and "where can I get the money to meet the last payment on my Mustang?" and "how in the world can I get rid of this horrid cold that has been plaguing me for the past six months?" — are *infinitely* more important to most people than most of the problems the various organs of local control that would flourish under a participatory democracy would deal with. The neighborhood school board might have to consider whether a particular history text should be used even though its references to sub-Saharan Africa were fleeting. Yet for most members of the community this question is of minimal concern compared to, "will I be rehired?," "how huge will the next doctor's bill be?," "will James call me for a date?," "what did I say to annoy Nancy the last time we went to the movies?," etc. (We deliberately picked a "racial" issue that could arouse a majority of the community. Our point would have been made even more clearly had we selected a problem which such a board might more typically be called upon to resolve, viz, ought the school to add a course in French to its curriculum.)

This strong predilection of most persons for the personal over the public is, I believe, a factor presenting one of the greatest threats to the success of the ideas of those who call for the implementation of participatory democracy. Regardless of the amount of time which seems to be at their disposal and regardless of their quantum of trust in the political system, the majority of persons give "public questions" a distant second place in their scheme of things. And common sense insists that one who is relatively much more concerned with his health or with retaining his job or with his popularity with his friends or even with his ability to break eighty the next time he goes to the golf course than he is with whether a job training program should be set up in his neighborhood or whether textbook A rather than textbook B should be adopted is not going to be too likely to pressure the local boards whose duty it is to resolve these problems.

Of course, it could be argued that many people whose concerns are mainly personal will nonetheless pay some attention to politics; and there are quite a few individuals who do fall into this category. But at least one study has shown that, at least in the case of individuals *deeply entangled* in their personal concerns, little notice is in fact taken of the social sphere. This study showed that persons with low-self esteem were not much interested in politics, while the opposite was generally true for persons with higher self-esteem. The author of the study, Morris Rosenberg, then asked why this should be the case, and concluded that it was so because persons with low self-esteem turned their attention inwards, and (this is the point that is important for our purposes) thus did not turn their minds to matters of social import. In fact, when the results of the study were "controlled" for the variable labelled concern personal problems, the difference in interest in public affairs between persons with high self-esteem and persons of low self-esteem was significantly narrowed.[14] (In other words, what Rosenberg did was to see whether the persons with high self-esteem and serious personal problems were much more interested in politics than the more common persons with low self esteem and serious personal worries; and whether the persons with high self-esteem and no serious personal worries were much more interested in politics than the persons with low self-esteem but no serious personal worries. The answer to both of these questions was "no," i.e., that serious personal problems tended to be accompanied by unawareness of the political sphere whether the respondent was a person of high self-esteem or low self-esteem, etc.)

Another attempt to rebut the position that putting more emphasis on personal than on social problems keeps people from participating in politics is that the pursuit of the solution of the personal will frequently lead to a solution of political problems. Charles Reich at one point in his *Greening of America* seems to be arguing somewhat along these lines.[15] His argument seems like a modernized version of the thesis of laissez faire economics that each person's pursuit of his enlightened self interest will produce the general welfare. Whether it is any more valid than the latter has to await the test of experience. Also, the anti-bureaucratic radicals could contend that individuals who are encouraged to discuss their personal problems with others will see that these worries are to a large extent caused by flaws in the social order and will then take an active interest in political matters. Something like this may be what is meant by the rather cryptic assertion in the Port Huron Statement that "the political order . . . should provide outlets for the expression of personal grievance and aspiration . . . ; channels should be commonly available to relate men to knowledge and to power so that private problems — from bad recreation facilities to personal alienation — are formulated as general issues."[16] However, whether community "encounter sessions" can actually become community "town meetings" must likewise await future determination.

Since we place so much emphasis on the danger to the realization of the decentralist socialists' ideals that arises from the fact that most people think far more about personal than about social problems, we should note in passing some of the studies indicating that men's minds do work this way. The most noted of these works is Samuel Stouffer's *Communism, Conformity and Civil Liberties*.[17] Stouffer's respondents were asked "What kind of things do you worry about most?," and 80% of these men and women answered solely "in terms of personal and family problems."[18] Forty-three percent of the sample were primarily concerned with what Stouffer labels "personal business or family economic problems," while another 24% indicated that their main fear involved

health, either their own or that of a member of their family.[19]
Typical answers were these (all to be read as prefaced by the
phrase "My main worry is").

> "I've been laid off three months. I'm worried about
> making a living. Doesn't seem to be much work. I worry
> I may lose my job, also, I might get sick."

> "My job. I'm just new at managing this chain store
> and I'm very concerned about it."

> "I'm going to have a baby and I worry about if it's
> going to turn out all right."

> "It's the polio season at the present time. . . . "

> "My marriage difficulties. I have just divorced my
> husband."

> "Living in town and I like the country but I married
> a town lady the second time. I need the country."

> "Money goes too fast. Food, it is so expensive. High
> rent. We're moving to California to see if we can get a
> better living there."[20]

The first six of the above comments clearly indicate that
the speakers' mental energies are primarily turned inward
upon themselves (and perhaps upon their families). One
might argue that answers such as the seventh show that that
interviewee's greatest worry *is* about a social problem, i.e.,
inflation. But when one is worried about a social phenomenon only because he perceives it as seriously affecting him
and when his only response to that phenomenon is to
grumble about it, to tamely submit to it, and/or to seek to
shield only himself and his family from its poisons, we cannot say that his fretting means that his mind is running on
political or social issues. What the last-quoted respondent is
reeally saying is "My main worry is that *I* don't have enough
money for the things I need" and not "My main worry is
that a good number of people in this country don't have the
cash to purchase the things they want." He who makes the
latter statement or who suggests how individuals generally
can blunt the effects of higher prices can be said to be

socially involved; but he who makes the former or its equivalent has made it clear that his major concerns are personal. (It is true, of course, that a lively interest in economics, may have developed because one had money problems in his youth and even that it may continue because he wants to avoid poverty in the future. But one who worries about his own pocketbook or the unbalanced budget of his family cannot be said to have any interest in economics unless he simultaneously devotes a good deal of thought to the causes of and remedies for empty pocketbooks in general!)

Robert Lane's *Political Ideology*,[21] a study of the political beliefs of fifteen residents of a city in the Eastern United States, backs up these findings of Stouffer. As he said in one place: "The lives of men of Eastport, like most Americans' lives, are much more concerned with the business of buying and selling, earning and disposing of things, than they are with the 'idle talk of politics.' "[22] And as he notes a bit later on,

> "Aside from psychic conflicts, the main sources of tension, the most difficult choices the men must make [are not created by politics but] are created by role conflicts, of which the central one is that between the role of husband and father . . . on the one hand and the role of workman . . . on the other. It arises, for example, in the decision on whether or not to take a second job, and, if one does, how to find the time to listen to and care about matters at home. Another such conflict is posed in the problem of how to be a good son to an aged parent living in the confines of a small apartment, or how to be a good husband to a wife with limited sympathy for a difficult oldster about the home."[23]

In short, Lane's work backs up the thesis that men are more troubled by their ulcers and wives than by the war in Vietnam or by the country's shortage of good, cheap housing; and that the man who broods over his quarrel with his office mate is much more typical than the man who loses sleep over Russia's 1968 invasion of Czechoslovakia.

We have noted above many obstacles which make men apathetic about the small scale institutions the participatory democrats favor. To reiterate, there is the lack-of-time dilemma; there is the possibility that the new institutions will concern themselves with issues of no importance or that their constituents will not perceive that what they are discussing is relevant to one aspect or another of their lives; there is the chance that the voters will feel suspicious of the men responsible for the creation of the new institutions or that an agency's proceedings and elections will not be well publicized or enlivened by debate; and finally, there is always the probability that people will take no manifest interest in what an agency is doing simply because they are more worried about personal problems. Now, as we have admitted, some of these obstacles (e.g., a lack of debatable issues) will not crop up too frequently, while others (e.g., lack of adequate publicity) can be eliminated without too much difficulty. But four of the others — the lack of time, the failure to perceive relevance, the worry about trivia, and the primacy of the personal over the public — are not only common but difficult to eliminate. Thus we must conclude that indifference about the organs of participatory democracy *is* a phenomenon that is highly likely to prevent these agencies from functioning as devices for making the majority of men self-governing. Almost all the small-scale institutions that we have considered have evoked a "couldn't care less" attitude from those who are supposed to participate in their control; and some of the causes of this passivity are recurrent and deep-rooted. And, as we contended before, the man who ignores the activities of an organization is certainly not self-governing as regards the policy it formulates.

There is one more point brought up by the considerations of this chapter that may be disheartening to the anti-bureaucratic radicals. We have noted many, many factors that could make an institution of participatory democracy a failure. In addition to those listed in the previous paragraph, we can add, for example, the possible elitism and the possible lack of education of the members of the body's legislature. Let us assume that each of these factors could individually easily be winnowed out. Still, the stubborn fact remains that their number is great. This being the case, it could be argued that even granted that the chances are slight that any particular one of them will adversely affect the relations between an institution of participatory democracy and its clientele, the chances that these relations will be poisoned by *at least* one of them are rather high. (The logic is similar to that which forces us to conclude though there is only about a sixteen percent chance that the New York Mets will win the championship of the six-team Eastern Division of the National Baseball League, a sixteen percent chance that the Philadelphia Phils will win it, a sixteen percent chance that the Chicago Cubs will win it and a sixteen percent chance that the Pittsburgh Pirates will win it, the chances are about sixty-five percent that this plum will fall either to New York, Philadelphia, Chicago or Pittsburgh.) Thus the institution's proceedings may be well publicized and its "legislature" may be responsive to the people and hold many lively debates on questions which its constituents feel are important and pertinent to their lives. But if, for example, most of these constituents are very busy people, the members of this legislature will not be hearing very often from them.

The partisans of decentralist socialism will no doubt make the following responses to all that has been asserted in this chapter and its two predecessors. This discussion of whether or not small-scale institutions are likely to be the instruments by which citizens are induced to influence as individuals the policy which affects them has assumed that these institutions will function in the sick welfare-state capitalism of today. But it is not inherent in human nature that men will behave in an elitist manner, feel themselves pressed for time because of the demands of work, be suspicious of the government, refuse to carry out the duties which they have been elected to perform, put the personal over the public, etc. It is not surprising, the participatory democrats would assert by way of example, that the individual now places a great deal of emphasis upon his personal problems. In a society where it is deemed an honor to make a profit for oneself, the average man will almost inevitably come to feel what happens himself is much more crucial than what happens to his neighborhood, city, state or country. The command "look to your own welfare exclusively in your economic life" is almost bound to be converted by the majority of the people into the broader doctrine that your own concerns are always more important than public issues. Moreover, they would continue, the society they want to create would emphasize fellowship and brotherly love, as well as work councils and neighborhood government. In such a context, it would be almost unthinkable that most people would care more about whether their Johnny was going to wed Mary than about whether a new small park should be built on the next street — or at least that they would let their worry over Johnny's marital problems prevent them from participating in the debate over the public park. It would likewise be beyond belief that most people would eschew such a debate because they wanted to finish a book or article or take an extended trip to Bermuda in mid-winter. Obviously, too, under such a state of affairs the policy making body of an institution such as a works council would in fact be public-spirited enough to make use of its legal prerogatives and to do so in accordance with the wishes which the majority of its citizens would certainly express. In short, to criticize participatory democracy because it will not produce self-governing individuals on the basis of evidence culled from a day and age when men's attitude toward life has been perverted by an evil economic order that places a premium on selfishness is, the advocates of decentralist socialism would contend, extremely unfair.

(One could anticipate, too, that these men would meet the retort that works councils in Yugoslavia have in may cases not resulted in the individual worker's participation in the development of factory policy with the rejoinder that though Yugoslavia is a socialist country a high percentage of those who have been workers since 1948 grew up in a partly feudal, partly capitalist and partly fascist society and thus are cursed with selfish attitudes and ways of behavior which are relics of this older system. They would add, moreover, that the new rulers of the country have not as yet been able to completely insulate the younger generation from the sad example of the older.)

It is true, of course, that in a society where men are essentially other-regarding participatory democracy might well have some success in terms of making the majority of men self-governing as individuals. Where many institutions of society are under the legal control of those whose lives they directly affect *and* where these persons feel so responsible to others that they are actively concerned with the way these institutions are functioning, it is certainly not at all utopian to contend that the majority of these persons will put pressure upon the institutions (e.g., a local public school) and that each member of this majority will be able to convince one member of the pertinent "legislature" (e.g., the community board of education having jurisdiction over that school) to vote this way or that on one or more issues facing it (e.g., should the "new math" be taught?, should an additional school building be constructed?, or should portable classrooms be added to the existing structure?). But it is doubtful that participatory democracy will be introduced into a society where the majority of persons are already altruists. No present-day nation can justifiably make such a claim about its citizenry — it is safe to assume that the high voter turnout in Russian elections and the numerous political discussion groups in China are phenomena which are the product of coercion by the state and not of any widespread, deep interest in things political resulting from concern for one's fellow man. Thus, were participatory democracy to be introduced tomorrow on a piecemeal or worldwide basis it would have to rely upon masses of men who would not be generous enough to set aside personal concerns, pressures, and inclinations in favor of giving serious attention to public problems.

To demonstrate this further, let us take a brief glance at the circumstances under which there is more than a totally negligible chance that participatory democracy would be introduced on a fairly wide scale in the modern world. It could be the child of a semi-socialist or genuinely reformist liberal government, such as those which have ruled England and Sweden in recent years or of an American administration headed by a man such as John Lindsay, the current Mayor of New York City. Here there would be few if any persons suspecting the motives behind the new policy — but there is no reason to believe that a few more years of social democratic rule in England will make the citizens of these nations significantly more other-regarding, and there is just as little reason to feel that the election of a Lindsay by the American people would necessarily be preceded by their conversion *en masse* to the cause of their fellow men. The same considerations are, of course, valid in the less likely event that institutions of participatory democracy were created by conservative regimes; and here there is the additional problem, already mentioned in our discussion of the community action programs of the war on poverty, that some of the minority groups in the country would suspect the new institutions as devices erected by the establishment to maintain its power by "buying off" its more militant opponents. (Actually a conservative administration might well engage in a few experiments in participatory democracy not to toss a bone to the restless masses but out of a sincere belief that problems can be solved better at the local level than in Paris, London or Washington. But these endeavors would still be greeted with scepticism by many.)

It is not completely inconceivable that some real attempts at workers' control of industry or neighborhood control of local institutions might be implemented by a communist regime. Recent history shows a communist government, especially one which takes power in a violent revolution, is for a period of time at least going to emphasize centralization in deed if not in word to insure that it will stay in power. But once the anti-communist groups have been effectively stamped out, the leaders may no longer feel the need to control everything from the center. Likewise, the mere fact that attempts at participatory democracy will have been made in non-communist nations may lead to popular clamor for similar reforms in the communist world (as may a study of the young Marx's writings on alienation in work and of some of the works of the communist and non-communist intellectuals who have interpreted and amplified upon these). Also, a communist nation which feels itself threatened by Russia or China may want to modify its socialism so as to distinguish it from the socio-economic system of these giants — the conflict with the Soviet Union is certainly one reason why Tito's Yugoslavia adopted workers' control of industry in the early 1950's. For all these reasons, then, some real participatory democracy is not out of the question in communist nations. However, there is no reason to think that the citizens of communist countries are any more public spirited than those in the non-communist world. The communists talk about their successes in creating "the new socialist man," but this seems little more than talk. (If it were more than propaganda, the Russians, for example, would not be having trouble getting people to voluntarily migrate to Siberia so that that part of the U.S.S.R. can rapidly be developed.) In other words, the residents of a Moscow, Sofia or Warsaw neighborhood that were, for example, given control over neighborhood schools and enterprises would not feel more deeply than their counterparts in London or Chicago that it was their duty to keep pressuring the neighborhood "legislature" to operate these institutions in a way that fit their vision of the public interest. In fact, one could argue with some degree of plausibility that the behavior of certain existing communist regimes has made people so suspicious of them that reforms under their sponsorship would be viewed with the scepticism with which many residents of Harlem in New York City would regard a measure of the Nixon administration placing local welfare offices in the hands of the local community.

We have accordingly, to say that if participatory democracy is to come into being in any nation in the near future its success probably will depend on men similar to those who were supposed to take part in the ongoing endeavors we have been depicting. That is, it probably will have to rely on persons who are more concerned with themselves than with public problems or who are too busy or who tend to ignore the wishes of those to whom they are responsible, etc. (We are, admittedly, overlooking at present the issue of whether participatory democracy will in and of itself be likely to make men other-regarding.) Therefore, we must stand firm in our conclusion that the likelihood of its success is slight, for if it is to make men self-governing, the legislatures of the new, small-scale institutions must not only govern wisely and responsively but their electorates must, as well, produce something which can be responded to!

There are two qualifications that must be made of the position taken in the above paragraph. Reich's *Greening of America* contends that we are on the verge of a mass revolution in human consciousness in which people will no longer be motivated by a desire to "get ahead" of their fellow men and to subordinate man to the state and society. They will, rather, emphasize beauty, creativity, imagination and responsibility to their fellow men in their scale of values.[24] If Reich is right, participatory democracy, which he himself appears to favor,[25] will become a perfectly feasible way of ordering society. Also Tom Hayden, in his book *Trial*,[26] urges the creation of more and more "islands" featuring a non-competitive, community-regarding life style in the midst of self-seeking, intolerant "average America." Examples of such communities are the "drop-out" and university areas of Madison, Ann Arbor, the Upper West Side of New York City, etc.[27] Once again, if these islands develop fully the standard of values that Hayden believes they already to some extent possess, *and* if their example proves contagious and spreads across the United States and the world, participatory democracy would in all likelihood prove successful. Whether Reich's large-scale revolution in consciousness is really imminent or whether Hayden's radical enclaves will soon cover a good part of the United States and/or the world and will be governed by the spirit of generosity and love, only time will tell.

FOOTNOTES TO CHAPTER VII

1. See Neal, Fred W., *Titoism in Action,* p. 157. Clark and Hopkins, *op. cit.,* note at p. 161 that some American community action programs are in fact dominated by "outside elites," too, e.g., public and private social agencies. Admittedly, these are a far cry from the Yugoslav Communist Party.

2. The poor relationship between the Polish councils and the old power structure is vividly described in André Babeau, *Les Conseils Ouvriers en Pologne,* (Paris: Librarie Armand-Colin, 1960) , especially at pp. 157-66, 187-92, 200-10, 217-24.

3. Presidence du Conseil — Secrétariat Général du Gouvernement, *La Courte Expérience des Conseils Ouvriers en Pologne,* (Paris: La Documentation Française, Notes et Etudes Documentaires, August 26, 1969, #2453, p. 26) .

4. Donovan, John, *The Politics of Poverty* (New York: Pegasus, 1967) , pp. 43-48, 54-57, 137.

5. Lipset, Seymour Martin, *Political Man,* (New York: Anchor Books, 1963) , p. 1.

6. *New York Times,* June 19, 1971, p. 1.

7. Archie Dykes, *Faculty Participation in Decision-Making,* p. 38.

8. *Ibid.,* p. 24.

9. *Ibid.,* p. 24.

10. *Ibid.,* p. 24.
11. *Participatory Democracy,* p. 29.
12. Neal, Fred W., *Workers' Management of Industry in Yugoslavia,* American Universities Field Staff Reports, S. E. European Series, Vol. 2, #3, 1954, pp. 4ff.
13. Dykes, *op. cit.,* p. 2.
14. See Rosenberg, Morris, *Self-Esteem and Concern with Public Affairs, Public Opinion Quarterly,* 26:201ff, Summer, 1962.
15. Reich, Charles, *Greening of America,* (New York: Bantam Books, 1971) at pp. 247-48.
16. Jacobs and Landau, *op. cit.,* p. 156.
17. Stouffer, Samuel, *Communism, Conformity and Civil Liberties,* (New York: Doubleday, 1955).
18. *Ibid.,* p. 59.
19. *Ibid.,* p. 62.
20. *Ibid.,* pp. 60-65.
21. Lane, Robert, *Political Ideology,* (New York: Free Press, 1962).
22. *Ibid.,* p. 25.
23. *Ibid.,* p. 32.
24. See Ch. 12 of *op. cit.*
25. See his article *"Issues for a New Society,"* New York *Times,* March 9, 1971, p. 37.
26. Hayden, Tom, *Trial,* (New York: Holt, Rinehart and Winston, 1970).
27. *Ibid.,* p. 158-160.

VIII

THE POSSIBLE BY-PRODUCTS
OF PARTICIPATORY DEMOCRACY

Until now, we have been assuming that the success or failure of participatory democracy depends on one thing only: whether its implementation will make the average man a self-governing citizen. That is, we have defined a successful participatory democracy as one in which the average constituent of the various small-scale institutions that will be created will continually keep in touch with his representatives on the legislatures of these institutions and individually convince them to vote his way on one or several issues. The situation which we have assumed as ideal would be as follows, at least in the area of public education in large cities: The city would be divided into school districts of e.g., 10,000 adults each; the district would be headed by an elective board of education of, say, ten members — each of whom would, of course, have about 1,000 constituents; each member would be in frequent contact with each of his constituents; each of these men and women would convince him that his or her view on a matter particularly close to his or her heart was the correct one; and at board meetings he would then vote in a manner consonant with these views. However, we have seen evidence in the last two chapters that this ideal state of affairs is somewhat utopian, especially because, for a variety of reasons, the majority of his constituents would never bother to get in touch with him or even inform themselves about the board's activities.

Another important question now arises. If the ideal described in the above paragraph were to be attained, might there be any dangerous "side-effects" that would partly or completely cancel out the admittedly desirable result of giving each man more control over his own life than he has now? It is indeed good that each man become a self-governing citizen; but if the attainment of this ideal would thwart the realization of others we would be faced with the difficult alternative of having to decide whether the game is worth the candle — that is, whether we would rather have self-governing citizens than effectuate these other goals. What we must do now, therefore, is to see whether there are in fact any values whose actualization the implementation of participatory democracy might endanger. The most sensible way to do this, in turn, is to glance in detail at a few ongoing or recent experiments with participatory democracy in order to see what, if any, are the accessory evils to which they have given rise. If an organ of participatory democracy has produced a particular misfortune, we have some evidence that the more widespread introduction of participatory democracy in the future may make this misfortune more common; though this point will, to avoid misunderstanding, be repeated again and again throughout this chapter, it would be totally unjustified to infer from the existence of one or two cause-and-effect relationships of this sort that participatory democracy will always or usually give rise to this flaw. Unfortunately, as we shall soon see, the relevant data that can be obtained from actual attempts to institute participatory democracy is rather sparse, and thus we shall have to supplement it by hopefully germane observations about the workings of large-scale democratic institutions such as city, state and provincial legislatures and governments. We shall then see whether a system of decentralist socialism can be set up in such a way as to prevent it from presenting us with unwanted by-products and also whether it may produce benefits that we have not yet mentioned. (Most of the points that will appear in this and the final chapter have been made elsewhere; but none of these prior discussions of the possible side-effects of participatory democracy is as complete as ours in discussing the reasons for the relation between system and product.)

As we have indicated previously, a form of workers' management of industry was introduced in Yugoslavia in 1952. In the three or four years after the passage of the Yugoslav works council law, which granted the new bodies a good deal of freedom in setting economic policies for their firm, prices and wages rose sharply even though productivity did not. For example, *Borba* mentioned that one enterprise made a profit of 138% in one of these years even though it carried out only 38% of its production plan for that year. Moreover, many enterprises began engaging in profitable but economically undesirable "consumers' goods" production.[1] As a result of these happenings, the government deprived the individual plants of the large amount of autonomy that had been theirs with respect to salaries, prices and production. But in 1961, each council was given the authority to determine what percentage of the firm's income after taxes should be distributed to its workers as wages. This led to a near economic disaster. During that year, productivity increased only 3.5% but personal income rose 23%.[2] A severe inflation set in; for example, in the last four months of that year the retail price of food increased by 25%.[3] These occurrences compelled the government to require that the country's firms employ a certain proportion of their profits as working capital and that plants paying wages out of line with productivity reduce them. For example, the works council of one Slovene steel works was forced to order an 11% decrease in the total wages fund, since in that plant in 1961 productivity had shown no improvement but wages had risen by 11%.[4]

In 1965 the government once again decided to give the individual firms and their works councils a great deal of discretion as to how their gross receipts should be allocated.

Once again, many councils voted pay rises and in the year 1966 personal earnings paid out by the country's enterprises rose 38%. Some councils tried to justify these increases by including the sales price of their unsold products in their annual income statements; but the state soon put an end to this particular bit of chicanery.[5]

The general significance of these inflationary steps taken by Yugoslav works councils will be discussed later. Let it be noted now, however, that this book is not contending that *all* the councils in that country behaved in this way or that bodies of this sort that might be set up in other nations would always fatten their constituents' pay envelopes in the absence of any increase in output per man. Certainly, for example, not all the "bonuses" obtained by the German *Betriebsräte* for the employees in their firms were economically unjustifiable.

Few English-speaking people know much about the Yugoslav and other works councils. However, one particular experiment with participatory democracy, the Ocean Hill-Brownsville school district in New York City, received worldwide publicity during the autumn of 1968. (Admittedly, most people, being then unaware of the concept of "participatory democracy," did not attach this label to this endeavor to improve the education of poor blacks and Puerto Ricans.) Ocean Hill and Brownsville are two Negro and Puerto Rican slum neighborhoods in Brooklyn. For numerous reasons, the children in these areas were getting a very poor education: their scores on reading tests were, for example, far below the national average. The City Board of Education accordingly acquiesced in a proposal by the Ford Foundation to set up an experimental demonstration district in Ocean Hill-Brownsville. A good deal of the policy-making for the schools in the district — just how much was unclear — was to be set by a governing board drawn mainly from the neighborhood plus the "unit administrator" it would employ, and not (as previously) by the City Board of Education and the City Superintendent of Schools. The local governing board, at least initially, consisted of twenty-four men and women, including eight persons elected by the parents of the school children in the area plus five community leaders chosen by the eight parent representatives. The elections for parent representatives were held in early August, 1967, and about one fourth of those eligible to do so voted.[6]

On May 7, 1968, the governing board ordered its unit administrator, Rhody McCoy, to "terminate the services" of six administrators and thirteen teachers then working in the district. It is unclear whether the board wanted the nineteen merely transferred out of the district or actually removed from the New York City school system,[7] though there is substantial evidence to support the view that all the local board wanted was the former, more moderate course of action.[8] However, no specific charges were filed against the nineteen at the time they were ordered transferred, and these men were never given the opportunity to defend themselves before the governing board.[9] It is also clear that a good number of the thirteen teachers were members of the teachers union, the United Federation of Teachers of the AFL-CIO, which had earlier aroused the antagonism of the governing board and which was to become its major opponent the following September. Even the New York Civil Liberties Union, one of the bitterest opponents of the UFT, admitted that at least four of the teachers were fired solely because they opposed the creation of the demonstration district,[10] and that the procedures which accompanied the transfer of the nineteen were unfair and violative of due process.[11]

The ten teachers who decided to contest their transfers were cleared of charges of incompetence by a Negro trial examiner who had previously been a judge. The governing Board still refused to allow the ten back into Ocean Hill-Brownsville and this conduct in turn triggered a short teachers' strike in early September, 1968. The day after the end of this strike, the hundred or so union teachers in the Ocean-Hill-Brownsville school district attempted to return to their schools. When they did so, some of them were jeered at by residents of the area and told that if they came back to the district they would be carried out in pine boxes.[12] Many were given no teaching assignments or time cards to punch. Pupils at one school were encouraged to leave for the day by some non-union teachers and members of the governing board.[13] And so the union called its second strike, which ended at the end of September.

However, the governing board continued to insist that the union teachers should not be given classes to teach. On October 9 at Junior High School #271

> "Members of the governing board, aggressive teachers and neighborhood militants who had been allowed into the building threatened union teachers, union and Board of Education observers and the assistant principal whom [New York City Superintendent of Schools] Donovan had told to run the school."[14]

Mr. Donovan then closed the school. When it reopened, the union went on strike again, this time for five weeks. (Once again, we are not contending that the conduct of the Ocean-Hill-Brownsville Board would be typical of the behavior of the organs of a nation which was organized according to the principles of participatory democracy; but merely that what happened at Ocean Hill indicates some possible by-products of such a system.)

Let us now consider what possible side effects of decentralist socialism are disclosed by the events and actions described so far in this chapter. What is revealed clearly by the Yugoslav works council experience is that there is a real danger that some of the institutions of participatory democracy will act in a parochial manner. (It must be understood that when we say throughout this chapter that participatory democracy will give rise to a certain mischief we mean that it will produce this only if satisfactory safeguards have not been erected.) That is, they may act so as to provide immediate benefits for the small group of people they represent irrespective of whether or not their doing so will hurt the larger community as a whole. Thus the Yugoslav councils boosted wages far beyond what was justified by increases in productivity even though these boosts sent prices spiralling. And if these price increases had gone unchecked, the nation would have suffered greatly, for two obvious reasons. In the first place, many consumers would have been unable to purchase commodities they desired. And, secondly, Yugoslavia's ability to sell goods to other countries, and thus acquire the currency she must have to buy some of the items she desperately needs, would have contracted almost to the vanishing point.

Actually, we could have predicted that some organs of participatory democracy would over-emphasize local needs even if we had not had before us the example of the Yugoslav councils, etc. Even in the democratically elected legislature of today (at least where there is little party discipline) the representative from a given district will often concern himself with satisfying the wants of that district regardless of whether doing so would be healthy from the point of view of the land as a whole. It could be argued that one of the reasons the United States of America refuses to curtail its overly-expensive defense program and begin doing more to end poverty is that every Senator or Congressman, no matter how emotionally opposed he is to the arms race, wants to see defense contracts and jobs continue to flow from Washington to firms and men and women in his own state or district. Senator X from the State of Dasota may be well aware that the naval shipyard in Dasotopolis is a waste of money and wholeheartedly committed to the idea that public funds should be used to rejuvenate the cities and guarantee everyone a decent standard of living. But just let the government propose to shut down that shipyard — Senator X will be in the thick of the fight to keep it open.

At least when a policy-making body represents the whole

of a relatively large entity (e.g., a nation, state, or city) there is good reason to believe that the parochialism of its individual members will not be permitted *full* sway. Thus the demand of Senator D that an aircraft factory in his state be given a lucrative contract to build a plane that will become obsolete as soon as it is put on the drawing boards may be thwarted by senators from other states. In this particular matter, they can not only see more clearly than Senator D, but they well know that in case that factory gets this contract some firms in their states will be deprived of some profitable business. But when a board represents only one factory or one neighborhood there may well be no factor operating within the board itself to check it when it becomes too locally inclined. Thus the Yugoslav councillors and their constituents can only benefit, at least in the short run, from doubling the take-home pay of the workers in the enterprise. Of course, there may be a few wise members of the council who are aware that actions like this will lead to an inflation which will quickly be disastrous for the country as a whole and which will ultimately injure their own constituents. (These, of course, will soon find that their doubled wages will buy less than the pittance which they formerly received. In addition, the nation may soon be out of foreign currency and if this happens the firm may be unable to purchase abroad a piece of capital equipment which it must have in order to keep running.) But there is no guarantee, of course, that the council will be blessed with men as far-seeing as this. Since they will all benefit in the short run by parochialism, they will be under no incentive to step back and contemplate its dangers.

The discharge of the nineteen teachers and administrators from Ocean Hill-Brownsville without informing them of the charges against them plus the subsequent threats to use violence against them, as well as the fact that the probable reasons for wanting them out of Ocean Hill-Brownsville included their membership in the United Federation of Teachers and/or their opposition to the demonstration district, indicates that some organs of participatory democracy may tend to ignore fundamental freedoms such as freedom of speech, freedom of association, and the right not to lose one's job without knowing the reasons why he is suffering this fate and without having the right to confront those who have accused him. Once again, a little thought will show us why this is the case. Under a system of participatory democracy, a good number of the new units are bound to be overwhelmingly or exclusively lower and lower middle class. Thus most of the factory employees who would select works councils would be drawn from these social classes, while many of the neighborhoods which would be given control of schools, etc. in the neighborhood would also be dominated by one or both of these groups. (Ocean Hill-Brownsville, for example, is predominantly working class.) Now research has shown that the lower and lower middle classes tend to be less respectful of fundamental freedoms than the middle and upper classes.[15] (This "working class authoritarianism" is not the product of extra original sin on the part of the poor, but due to environmental factors such as leaving school early and the greater likelihood of a working class child's being exposed to physical violence in the home. The lack of education makes it difficult for them to understand the rather abstract justification for tolerance while the exposure to physical violence makes them readier to accept it rather than discussion as a way toward solving disputes.)[16] Thus a board which was elected by a working class community would have little reason from a political point of view to respect those values which are incorporated into a document such as the Bill of Rights of the American Constitution. It would not lose many friends in such a community by firing persons who aroused its ire without giving them any opportunity to explain their course of action: in fact, if it appeared to give the "oddball" too much of a break, it might find the anger of the community directed at it.

On the other hand, a legislature representing the whole of a city, state or nation will have men elected by middle class constituencies as well as members from working class areas. The former group will be responsible to people who will be suspicious of arbitrary or tyrannical behavior — or, more accurately, they will find that there exist articulate interest groups (e.g., the American Civil Liberties Union) in their districts who will be fervently opposed to violations of the right of freedom of speech, freedom of association, etc. Therefore these particular respresentatives will have good reason not to permit their legislature to behave too lawlessly. Moreover, a member from a working class district in such a legislature who is personally "pro-civil liberties" is more likely to vote that way under these circumstances than if he were a member of a board having jurisdiction solely over his constituency. In the first place, his basic predispositions will be reinforced by hearing the arguments of those from more "liberal" communities. And, secondly, he knows that it will be difficult for his constituents to blame him personally for any "excessive" adherence by his legislature to basic freedoms, for he will often be able to say to them that given the composition of the legislature, an "anti-civil liberties" vote would have been a futile thing, anyway.

There is one more reason why in the United States the percentage of the organs of participatory democracy that would tend to ignore fundamental freedoms would probably be higher than the similar figure for policy-making bodies that were drawn from a relatively large community. This is that some of these organs would be representative of areas composed of minority groups such as blacks and Mexican Americans that have suffered and are suffering degrading and insulting treatment at the hands of many whites. These minority groups are, accordingly, gripped by anger and mistrust and are not unlikely to elect individuals with these feelings to the neighborhood organizations that would govern the community under a system of participatory democracy.

And persons who, justifiably or not, are outraged at and suspicious of a certain class of people may find it difficult to
permit the members of this class to express their own point
of view or to subject them to penalties such as the loss of
a job only after objectively weighing all the evidence pro
and con. As Lipset says, "High states of tension require immediate alleviation, and this is frequently found in the vent-
ing of hostility against a scapegoat . . . "[17]

The last paragraph naturally leads us to our next problem.
One tactic employed by the United Federation of Teachers
in the 1968 New York City teachers' strikes we have mentioned is that the governing board of Ocean Hill-Brownsville
was anti-white and/or anti-Semitic. This was untrue — seventy percent of the new teachers hired by the board were
white, and perhaps forty to fifty percent were Jewish.[18] Nonetheless, those who have criticized the 1969 act splitting New
York City into about thirty separate school districts each controlled by its community on the ground that the new boards
would countenance racial or religious bigotry in hiring and
curriculum are not being totally irrational. There is a danger
that in a society such as the United States which is ethnically
heterogenous the introduction of participatory democracy
would create institutions which tended to manifest, encourage or condone race hatred. The reasons for this lie partly
in what we noted when we contended that participatory democracy might breed intolerance of dissent and a scorn for
fair procedures, e.g., the fact that many of these organs would
be elected by overwhelmingly lower and lower-middle class
constituencies. These classes are somewhat more intolerant of
persons of different races and religious than are the middle
and upper classes,[19] as can be witnessed by the success of the
segregationist George Wallace among American workers in the
1968 and 1972 presidential campaigns and by the popularity
among the London dock workers of the racist British M.P.
Mr. Enoch Powell. (By the way, Powell was a Professor of
Classics, which should make it clear that we are speaking

only in generalities and that many well-educated citizens are bigots and many manual workers are not.)

But there is a broader reason why neighborhood-based organs of participatory democracy might in an ethnically pluralistic society refuse to hire persons of a certain race or religion, deny benefits to any member of these groups, encourage the teaching of the supremacy of one race or another in the local schools, etc. In the United States the members of an ethnic group often choose to or are forced to live in the same neighborhood. Thus we have Italian areas, Irish areas, Jewish areas, Mexican areas, Puerto Rican areas, and huge Negro ghettoes. Consequently, many of the communities which would choose the neighborhood "legislatures" would be dominated by one ethnic group. Accordingly, the members of these boards would find it politically profitable to employ members of this group only, to refuse to counteract racist statements made by the local teachers, etc. It goes without saying that this consideration is valid for white as well as black, for Jew as well as gentile. There is a real danger that a school board elected by Jewish or Italian middle class homeowners will accept as teachers only Jews or Italians and will not crack the whip when these teachers tell their pupils that Negroes must be kept out of the area at all costs or that Jews (Italians) are the "herrenvolk" — just as there is a real danger that a Negro school board will rehire some militant teacher who urges his students to burn down white owned shops in their community. In short, James Madison was correct when he said in *Federalist* X that by *enlarging* the area of the political unit one would increase the number of groups in that unit and that such an increase would mean that no one group would be likely to seize control of the government and use it for its own selfish ends. A school board representative of, e.g., all New York City will not tolerate overt bigotry by its teachers; but one elected from, e.g., an all-Jewish or all-Italian or all-Negro community is somewhat more likely to do so. It is very true that the first school board elections

under the 1969 New York school decentralization law produced few, if any, boards completely by one ethnic group;
but this, springs from the fact that few of the districts it
created are ethnically homogeneous, a situation which arises,
in turn, because they are too large to please many participatory democrats.[20]

Some could argue that in the previous paragraphs we are
showing certain desirable as well as certain undesirable
consequences of the devolution of political, etc. power to
small groups. Most readers of this book would admit that it
would be unfortunate if decentralist socialism led to the hiring of teachers and other public employees who preached
racial and religious intolerance: the example of Catholic-
Protestant violence in Belfast, Northern Ireland, shows us
what happens when a city is divided physically along ethnic
or religious lines and each area harbors numerous individuals
who continually express their detestation of the groups that
inhabit other quarters of the city. But it could be argued
that there is really nothing wrong with a situation in which
a black community board in a black area hires only black
policemen, and teachers, a Jewish commuity board in a Jewish area hires only Jewish policemen and teachers, assuming
further that the black policemen, teachers, etc. do not spend
their time downgrading whites; the Jewish policemen and
teachers do not spend their time downgrading blacks, etc. In
fact, it has been argued that this state of affairs in which
only blacks will work with blacks, only Jews with Jews, only
Italians with Italians, etc. makes sense, since the members of
one ethnic group cannot really understand the problems of
another, even if, as is unlikely to be the case, they make a
genuine attempt to rid themselves of their prejudices against
the other.[21] One cannot deny that this argument has some
force; but it would take a separate book to give it the
thorough analysis it deserves. Suffice it to say here in partial
rebuttal that hiring on ethnic or racial grounds (except perhaps to insure that a group which has suffered discrimination

in the past gets a certain percentage of a certain type of position) is illegal under American and British legislation and (when done by a public agency in America) is unconstitutional as well under the Supreme Court's doctrine that racial classifications in a law are highly suspect.[22] Also, aside from the legal and constitutional issues, hiring exclusively along racial lines might well deprive e.g., the children of the area of excellent teachers drawn from other groups. Moreover, for a highly qualified person to apply for a position and to be told that he cannot get the job because he is black, Jewish, Italian, Irish, Armenian, etc. is, from a personal point of view, a highly demoralizing experience.

The critics of New York City's school decentralization make yet another point which is pertinent for our purposes, though one in all fairness cannot say that the Ocean Hill experiment or the workings of the 1969 law gives us any evidence in its favor. This is that even though the local school boards would not countenance bigotry their existence would make impossible the integration of the public schools. More generally, the argument is this: that in an ethnically heterogeneous nation the introduction of community control of institutions located in the community will make the mixing of ethnic groups less likely. The truth in this proposition is most evident from the following hypothetical. Assume that an American city of between 500,000 and 1,000,000 is divided up into fifty or so completely independent and autonomous school districts. Given residential patterns in American cities of this size, most of these districts would have jurisdiction over a largely all-white or largely all-black student body. There would not exist any central agency to, e.g., arrange to bus black students to a predominantly white school. Moreover, it would probably involve a great deal of paperwork before a student living in the area under the jurisdiction of one board could be transferred to a school under the jurisdiction of another, and most parents would be discouraged from attempting such a transfer simply because it would mean so many forms to fill out. But it is easy to visualize other examples, too, of how participatory democracy could keep different ethnic groups apart. Thus if the personnel who work out of neighborhood welfare offices are assigned to a particular office by a state or city agency, the city or state can see to it that at each office there is a good mixture of black and white workers, which in turn would facilitate contact between black and white professionals of this type. But if local welfare offices were under the control of neighborhood groups the chances are that few white workers would apply to work in an office in a black area and that few blacks would apply to work in an office in a white community. And this analysis is just as valid for a situation where the persons to be hired are policemen rather than social workers.

The foregoing assumes, of course, not only that legally-required segregation of ethnic groups is undesirable, but that "voluntary" segregation is as well. While almost all advocates of decentralist socialism would agree with the U.S. Supreme Court in *Brown v. Board of Education*[23] and subsequent cases that the former is dangerous, some would say that the latter is harmless or even beneficial (especially in the case of American blacks). In the words of one writer: "Currently the drive for full integration into American life is no longer perceived by many black people as being a possibility in the immediate future. Thus the drive has come for community control of those areas where blacks reside. It is a movement to allow black people to experience majority status and to make significant decisions affecting their lives which heretofore have been made by a majority apathetic or hostile to their aspirations. Community control would build black power by providing a locus for organization and through the concentration of resources . . . "[24] Once again, it is outside the scope of this book to solve the problem of integration versus voluntary segregation of ethnic groups. For personal reasons, the author of this book is biased in favor of the former, but he may be wrong. There is some evidence, cer-

tainly, that on the particular question of whether de facto
all-black or majority-black schools further or hinder the education of black children, those who believe that they impede
education are in the right. As the United States Commission
on Civil Rights found in a recent study:

"The outcomes of education for Negro students are
influenced by a number of factors including students'
home backgrounds, the quality of education provided
in their schools, and the social class background of their
classmates. In addition to these factors, the racial composition of schools appears to be a distinct element.
Racial isolation in the schools tends to lower students'
achievement, restrict their aspirations, and impair their
sense of being able to affect their own destiny.

By contrast, Negro children in predominantly white
schools more often score higher on achievemeent tests,
develop higher aspirations, and have a firmer sense of
control over their own destinies."[25]

There is one danger in participatory democracy that is
clearly revealed by *both* the problems with Yugoslav works
councils and those with the Ocean Hill-Brownsville school
decentralization experiment. To recapitulate, some Yugoslav
councils increased wages more than was socially desirable and
the Ocean Hill-Brownsville board dismissed some teachers
without giving them the opportunity to defend themselves
and, in the case of some of them, because they took a political position opposed to the boards. We have seen earlier
that these courses of action reveal that participatory democracy could produce behavior that would hurt that community as a whole as well as violations of fundamental rights.
But they show something else too: that there is a risk that
the new institutions will either unjustifiably ignore the producer for the supposed benefit of the consumer or unjustifiably ignore the consumer for the supposed benefit of the
producer.

Let us delve into this point a bit more deeply. As we implied in Chapter II, Guild Socialists such as G. D. H. Cole pointed out that there are two types of relationships in which one can stand with respect to a particular good or service. One can be a consumer (user) of the commodity (which we shall assume to be a car), or one can be a producer thereof.[26] (Cole was well aware of the case of the man who works in the car factory who wants to buy one of the vehicles he has helped produce. However, such an individual would pose no particular problem to him as he would just contend that during working hours the employee was a producer and that while selecting, driving and paying for the vehicle he was a consumer.) Now it hardly takes much reflection to see that in some respects, at least in the short run, the interests of producer and consumer may conflict. The consumer wants a quality car at low prices. Now this can be achieved several ways, but each of these involves some sort of disadvantage to the owner of the firm, to its employees, or both. One way to achieve the low price is through the payment of low wages; another involves the relinquishment by the owners of a desire for high profits; yet a third involves a combination of the first two means. One way to obtain a high quality car is through more reliance on work by individual employees and less on assembly line methods; but this will almost certainly involves an increase in the cost per car produced and thus a reduction of profit and/or wages if the less efficient but more satisfactory method is to be introduced without jacking up the cost. Another involves the rigorous inspection and testing of each vehicle as soon as it leaves the assembly line; this alternative, too, will mean a lessening of profit or wages if it is not to produce an increase in cost. On the other hand, the workmen want high wages; and one way to get this is to increase sales prices. Likewise, the shareholders want high profits, and, especially in an oligopolistic industry, this can easily be accomplished in the same way. (The phenomenon of labor and management combining against the consumer is a common one in all industrialized capitalist societies.) In addition, the workers want improved conditions of work, which once again can be financed out of the consumer's pocketbook. The workers also want to work less hard; and if they obtain this goal the real cost of each car will rise and, moreover, the desirable inspections and rechecks may no longer be carried out. And so on and so forth.

In Yugoslavia, those works councils which increased wages much more quickly than their work forces increased productivitiy had to boost their prices significantly. Consequently this sort of conduct can be labelled unjustifiably "anti-consumer" as well as "overly parochial". On the other hand, when the governing board at Ocean Hill-Brownsville asked that the nineteen teachers leave the district, its course of action can be viewed not only as violative of fundamental rights but as objectionably "anti-producer". From an economic and political point of view, teachers are as much producers as are workers in Ford's River Rouge, Michigan plant. If, say, a national organization of car buyers fired the workers in this plant without even attempting to justify this step we would have an example of wrongful anti-producer conduct; and the same is true where a school board discharges or transfers teachers without giving them a chance to defend themselves or because it doesn't like the latter's political views or organizational affiliations. Likewise, from a political and economic point of view, public school students are "consumers" of education. Thus if the teachers decided to force their pupils to conform to absurdly strict dress regulations, they would have enacted an overly anti-consumer measure. (An unfairly wrongful, etc. anti-consumer measure is one which significantly increases profits or wages without increasing productivity, which significantly dilutes the quality of a product, which increases the prices of a necessary commodity beyond the consumers' ability to pay, or which deprives him of rights such as freedom of speech and the right to a hearing. An unfairly wrongful, etc. anti-producer step is one which worsens his conditions of work, deprives him of his job, reduces his salary or denies him a deserved promotion without giving him the chance to be heard in his own behalf, or penalizes him because of his political affiliation, ethnic background, religion, or failure to conform to the life style adopted by the majority of his fellow citizens.)

Naturally, not every measure that adversely affects a consumer can be called unfairly anti-consumer and not every step that adversely affects a producer can be called unfairly anti-producer. For example, if the Yugoslav works councils upon which we have been concentrating in this chapter had raised wages only ten percent while productivity had risen six percent, it is arguable that this boost would not have been unjustifiably anti-consumer, even though it would increase the prices he had to pay, simply because the wages previously received by the workers had been just enough to keep themselves and their families alive. If the Ocean-Hill Brownsville Board had sought to rid themselves of the nineteen teachers on the basis of good evidence showing they were anti-Negro and had given them a real opportunity to rebut this charge, even the union would have had to confess that the board was not being unjustifiably anti-producer. All that we are saying here is that the Ocean Hill and Yugoslav experiments with participatory democracy demonstrate that one is not tilting at windmills when he contends that the implementation of the theories of the anti-bureaucratic radicals could lead in some instances to unjustifiably anti-consumer or anti-producer policies. (Just to keep the record straight, there are obviously many instances when it is unclear when e.g., an action which hurts producers is culpably anti-producer. Suppose the nineteen teachers had been recommended for a transfer on the ground that the evidence clearly demonstrated that their pupils were performing more poorly on reading tests than pupils in the same grades in the same schools who were instructed by other men and women and that the nineteen had been given the chance to explain this testimony away. Whether their transfer would be a step that we could call unjustifiably anti-producer would have to be determined by weighing the benefits to the students from getting new teachers for them against the inconvenience suffered by the teachers as a result of transfer on grounds of lack of success.)

It is one of the greatest theoretical weaknesses of the varied spokesmen for that disparate group we are calling the "decentralist socialists" or the "participatory democrats" that they make no suggestions about how to insure that the institutions of participatory democracy they wish to see established will strike some sort of fair balance between the needs of the producer and the needs of the consumer. Actually, this failing goes even deeper, for they generally (Eric Fromm is one exception) [27] do not even *see* that a conflict between the interests of the two may arise.[28] Thus the Black Power advocates who demand that the neighborhood control the local welfare office and police station never realize that the community, in order to get more help from the social workers and more protection against criminals, may try to achieve this end by lengthening the hour of the work day or shortening vacation periods. Other routes would cost money, and, as we shall see, many neighborhoods will be strapped for money. If consumers cooperatives were set up in any area, slum or Park Avenue, under the control of the citizens of that area, there might be a tendency to insist that the clerks and so on who worked in these enterprises spend long hours at the job in exchange for low wages — this would be one way to reduce the price of food and clothing. And student control of college faculty hiring and firing might result in a situation in which professors would have to teach six courses a semester — in which case they would have no time for research and little time for course preparation. Of course, as a preceding chapter noted, at present the faculty, i.e., the producers, have in practice the final say about matters such as what courses are to be taught. As most students (i.e. the consumer) would tell you, as a result of this practice many courses for which there is a demand are not taught at all, or are offered once every three or four years, or are given at the same hour as some useless course that the faculty believes should be required.

Why bodies such as the Ocean Hill governing board and the Yugoslav works councils are more likely to be overly anti-producer or overly anti-consumer than e.g., the government of a city, is simple to explain. It is true that the state, local and national governments of today have overlooked in the past and may be shunning in the present the justifiable claims of producer or consumer. But these institutions represent considerable numbers of producers and, it goes without saying, a multitude of consumers. Hundreds of thousands of city employees live in New York City and thus the local politicians cannot be entirely unreceptive to their demands. State, city and national legislators not only represent many workers and businessmen, but often depend upon money and campaigning from these sources to remain in office. But these senators, councilmen, etc. cannot totally ignore the consumer either, for every one of the persons who casts a vote for them is a consumer. On the other hand, the world the decentralist socialists would like to see come into being seems to be based largely upon groupings which are wholly composed of producers — the works councils, or almost entirely made up of consumers — the city neighborhood. It is not probable, for example, that a local school board elected by the neighborhood will be almost entirely responsible to "consumers" — the parents of children in public schools. The number of teachers under the board's jurisdiction will be minimal, and in any event those teachers in its schools who live outside the neighborhood will probably have no say in the selection of the board. And it is for these reasons that the organs of participatory democracy are more likely to ally themselves entirely with the producer (consumer) against the consumer (producer) than is the type of political system to which we are accustomed.

One possible weakness of participatory democracy not suggested as yet by any actual experiment with this sort of social system but which any student of local government or public administration would be quick to point out is that certain of the services which the participatory democrats would like the local community to render just cannot be provided adequately on a small-scale basis, (*This* danger is posed by any small unit — not just by small units democratically controlled). Education, libraries and other services require relatively large capital investments. The more people served by a library or school system, the less the per capita cost of operating that system and the more feasible it becomes for that system to offer a wide range of services. Accordingly, library and school systems located entirely within small towns usually cost more *per capita* than they do in large cities; and most small towns would find it utterly impractical to operate a high school with a wide range of language and vocational courses or a library with several hundred thousand volumes. We cannot avoid the conclusion that this sentence would be just as valid were the phrase "city neighborhoods" substituted for "small towns."

We have seen, therefore, that the organs of participatory democracy, even if they would make men self-governing citizens, might be somewhat more likely than the democratically elected governments of today to perform certain tasks inefficiently, to unduly favor the local at the expense of the national, to turn a deaf ear to or actually engage in racial bigotry or violations of fundamental freedoms, to make it more difficult for men with different backgrounds to come to know one another and work together, and to violate the rights of the producer or the consumer. Note, again, that we are not saying that participatory democracy *would* have these adverse consequences, but merely that it *could* and that unless precautions were taken, it would be a bit more likely than extant democratic political systems to produce these obnoxious side effects. Obviously, democratically elected legislatures have been guilty of bigotry — take any southern United States state legislature and city council between 1880 and 1965. However, it should be mentioned that the electorate here was analogous to the type of electorate that would select "neighborhood" legislatures. Since the customs of the community excluded Negroes from the franchise and since the white south was, on the whole, Anglo-Saxon and Scotch-Irish Protestant, its electorate was relatively and culturally homogeneous. (The liberal Mississippi editor Hodding Carter recognized this relative uniformity, commenting that "Nowhere outside the British Isles is there so large a concentration of people of English and Scotch-Irish ancestry as in the South . . . Of our approximately 28 million white people, more than 95% have these common origins . . . ") [29]

The advocates of participatory democracy might well respond to this list of conclusions that the mere fact that severe risks attend a political or other enterprise which promises substantial benefits is no reason why the project should be discarded. Queen Isabella of Spain financed Columbus' journey across the Atlantic even though there was a very real chance it would end up as a waste of life and money. More seriously, American independence from Britain was certainly fraught with numerous dangers. It was not at all certain whether, deprived of the protective blanket of the British armed forces and navy, the thirteen colonies could keep from fighting one another or from succumbing to French or Spanish invasions. It was also a risk when the framers of American Constitution opted to give the people some say in government rather than to create pure oligarchy, an oligarchic monarchy, or an absolute monarchy. Never since the end of classical civilization had the inhabitants of a polity of substantial size been accorded even this much political power; and it was far from certain that they could employ it wisely.

It is true that the fact that there are visible risks in an attempt at restructuring society should not of itself induce us to forget about the venture. On the other hand, it would be senseless to ignore the fact that the implementation of a new social order such as participatory democracy may have some

unhappy by-products even if it gives men more share in setting the policy that touches upon their lives. Not only does
this contingency have to be taken into account when we decide the shape which we would like the society of the future
to assume but, just as importantly, in case we do opt for
participatory democracy, knowledge of these possible dangers
will enable us to take certain steps which will render them
less likely to occur. The question now posed for us is thus
this one: if a country decides to wholeheartedly implement
participatory democracy, how can it have its cake and eat
some of it too; i.e., how can it make sure that the organs
which will (hopefully) make men more self-governing will
not abuse their prerogatives in the ways already described in
this chapter.

The answer is an easy one — at least in theory. Every non-
totalitarian country has certain institutions which serve as
a check on the unjust actions of others, and there is no reason
why these cannot be employed to restrain the organs of participatory democracy when these behave wrongfully. (In general the following discussion will use examples drawn from
the United States of America; but, slightly modified to accord
with the structure of the relevant political system, it is applicable to any country.) One set of institutions which can
clamp down on the new neighborhood governments, etc. is
the courts. The American federal and state courts will issue
injunctions preventing city and state governments or any
public or quasi-public institution from depriving individuals
of their right to speak or of their right not to be discriminated
against on account of their race, creed or color. The judiciary
could, accordingly, order a neighborhood school board to rehire or compensate a teacher whom it fired for saying something that met with its displeasure. In fact, under the United
States Constitution as it is presently interpreted by the Supreme Court, the judiciary would *have* to issue such an order.
Likewise, if a school board in a white lower middle-class area
of a big city refused to hire Negroes, the courts would order
it to cease this sort of discrimination.

Thus the courts would be good devices for preventing the organs of participatory democracy from engaging in acts of bigotry or in other invasions of fundamental rights. Even in England and other countries without a written constitution they could be useful in this respect if they interpreted the statutes setting up these organs to prohibit these types of behavior. They would be less satisfactory as means for keeping the local bodies from taking steps that would benefit the small community at the expense of the state or national economy or which would hurt producers (consumers) unduly. Thus the question of whether or not the prices charged by a works-council controlled factory are too high is not really one which a court can answer in the absence of some aid from the legislative or executive — and the same can be said about the problem of whether a locally-managed consumers co-op requires its employees to work overly long hours. But this consideration itself indicates to us that the economic parochialism or the excessive producer (consumer) orientation of the organs of participatory democracy can be kept under check by the legislatures and the executive branches of higher levels of government — i.e., of the city, state (province) and nation. One way these higher levels can protect the nation in economic matters is simply to pass laws preventing the agencies of participatory democracy from engaging in certain conduct. Accordingly, the national government could enact maximum hours of work legislation applicable to all enterprises in the country, even to cooperatives run by a board elected by the community the co-op serves. In fact, the Yugoslav government was able to combat the inflationary activities of its works councils simply by depriving them, at least temporarily, of certain powers over wages and prices. An administrative department could command a firm to stop fabricating an un-needed product or to stop polluting the air. National, state, etc. legislation can, of course, also be a device for insuring that local boards eschew bigotry and denials of fundamental freedoms.[30] Thus the United States government has at times passed statutes making it illegal for any public official to deny a person his fundamental rights.

There is perhaps even a better mechanism that the higher legislatures can use to insure that the organs of participatory democracy behave. It has not escaped the attention of some decentralist socialists that just about all of the activities which it wants to place in the hands of the local community or work group to control are expensive. Few neighborhoods, rich or poor, in the United States can support a decent school system unaided. Even wealthy communities in suburban Nassau county in New York State depend at least in part on federal and state funds to operate their schools. Likewise, practically all the neighborhood school boards that would be established under a system of participatory democracy would depend on city, state and federal monies for survival. Some (such as Ocean Hill) would be more dependent than others, but none could continue to operate the schools without a grant from above. Likewise, welfare offices, police stations, etc. that would be run by neighborhood governments would need this sort of aid.[31] Even enterprises organized along lines of participatory democracy which would sell goods and services rather than provide them *gratis,* cannot function independently of the larger community. Most of the raw material purchased by a democratically run factory, for example, will have to come from another enterprise.

Since every organ of participatory democracy will need some cooperation from other institutions and, more specifically, those that offer free or financially unprofitable services will need some money from higher levels of government in order to continue to satisfactorily perform these services, one more solution to the problem of the errant local agency (especially when that agency is a neighborhood government) is obvious. By threatening to cut off the supply of life-giving aid from that body, the superior legislature can compel it to cease racial discrimination, reduce its prices, treat its workers fairly, etc. The pattern already exists in most nations. In

Britain and America, for example, the higher levels of government give billions of dollars or pounds to the lower. But their grants are not unconditional, and may be withdrawn if the recipient behaves in such a way as to make less likely the realization of the ends for which the grants were appropriated or in other ways which the grantor deems undesirable. Thus American cities will not receive money from the national government for slum clearance unless the plan which they have drafted is approved by the national government, and the money will be cut off if the city begins departing from that scheme. Likewise, under the U.S. Civil Rights Act of 1964, no state or city agency may continue to receive federal funds if it discriminates against anyone on racial, etc. grounds. As a result of this provision, quite a few school districts in the American south have decided to integrate their formerly segregated schools. Needless to say, this clause can be applied as well to any neighborhood school board or welfare agency that practices racial segregation.

Some anti-bureaucratic radicals would object to this argument about financial compulsion — even though it helps them by indicating that there are devices to prevent neighborhood legislatures from engaging in ruthless or excessively parochial behavior. They would contend that under their vision most services would be provided by neighborhood bodies and consequently the activities of the state, city, and national governments would be minimal. This being the case, the neighborhoods would be able to tap a great deal of money for themselves that is now taken by the more remote political systems, especially by the national government. Consequently, these small polities would be financially independent. To this two answers can be given. Some neighborhoods are so poverty stricken at present (e.g., Harlem, Bedford Stuyvesant, Watts, Chicago's south side or little Appalachia, Glasgow's Gorbals) that even if neighborhood governments were the only taxing organs in the country, the community could not afford decent schools, police protection, welfare services, libraries, etc. Secondly, there seems to be a tendency for sub-units (e.g., cities, states) of a larger political system to avoid taxing their citizens for as long as this is humanly possible. Admittedly, to some extent this tendency arises from a fear of driving out business, and, under the socialist system postulated by the participatory democrats, enterprises will not be conducted for a profit and thus will not threaten to flee the community when it increases its taxes. But it also is the result of a fear of inciting hard working, stable citizens to move to another unit; and one can expect that the local boards will be reluctant to tax because of this particular worry. Accordingly, it is likely that even under a system of participatory democracy, at least during the first few decades of its existence, much of the financial support for community institutions will have to come from above; and, as long as this is the case, the higher levels will be able to use the ploy of threatening to cut off aid in the event of malfeasance.

Of course, the various checks upon the local organs of participatory democracy may prove inadequate. On the other hand, they can work too well, i.e., in such a way as to defeat the intent behind the creation of this socio-economic system. The use of the courts, legislation, and threats to cut-off aid can take a form which will deprive the community legislatures of all their autonomy and thus make a mockery of the claim that the new state of affairs gives political authority to a body over which the average citizen can exert some control. In other words, too much interference from above can transform a system of decentralist socialism, where most policy is made by small units, into one of centralist socialism, where policy is made at the center. But the problem of maintaining the relative independence of the parts while at the same time preventing them from behaving in such a way as to threaten the well-being of the whole is one inherent in any political system where power is shared by two or more levels of government.[32] Nor can it be said that attempts to achieve such an equilibrium between whole and parts have always ended with the elimination of the prerogatives of the latter. In England, for example, local education authorities have a great deal of power even though most of their money comes from parliament and even though parliament could abolish the local authorities any time it pleased. And in the United States the states still have a great deal of freedom to experiment in the areas of, e.g., criminal law, education, health and welfare even though their performance of all these functions is subject to federal statutory and constitutional limitations and even though they receive conditional federal assistance in the areas of health, education and welfare. For example, if New York State were to decide that high school students could get academic credit for working in government offices, its schools would still continue to receive federal assistance. Accordingly, we cannot say *a priori* that the organs of participatory democracy democracy will become mere puppets if the higher levels of government retain their power to insure that they do not behave tyranically or parochially, and so defending participatory democracy by this somewhat paradoxical method of pointing to some of the possible controls upon it seems to be perfectly proper.

Not every device for insuring that the organs of participatory democracy account themselves properly need make use of ukases from higher levels of government. We could supplement these orders from above with a procedure under which these various organs could check one another. For example, we could provide that a factory governed by a works council set prices only in conjunction with a body selected by (a) the works councils of the enterprises that purchase from it and (b) the neighborhood boards that control the cooperative stores which sell its products. This requirement would make it much less likely that the factory works council would set fantastically high prices in order to get higher wages for its constituents. Likewise, we could require that the workers in every local cooperative enterprise or group of local cooperative enterprises be allowed to have a works coun-

cil of their own and that their wages be fixed through negotiations between this council and the governing boards of the
cooperatives. And we could set similar rules for determining
the wages of the employees of local school boards, locally-
operated welfare agencies, etc.

Shaping our system of participatory democracy along these
lines would, of course, be of most help in the direction of
insuring that the new institutions would respect the interests
of both producer and consumer. It would also in theory prevent them from engaging in racial or religious bigotry or from
depriving persons of fundamental rights: presumably the
works councils in the cooperatives, the schools, etc. could obtain the power to have some say over hiring and firing and
exercise this power in order to prevent the elected boards
from discharging people on racial, religious or political
grounds. But there is, of course, nothing close to a guarantee
that these works councils would use these prerogatives for
these purposes and not just limit themselves to fighting for
higher wages and better working conditions. To insure that
the small-scale legislatures of participatory democracy (e.g.,
neighborhood government) treat equally qualified candidates
equally and respect the fundamental freedoms of speech,
press, association and fair hearing, it would thus not be
enough to have them confronted by these other small-scale
legislatures (e.g., works councils); they would, as well, have
to continue to be subordinate to the courts and legislatures
of the higher levels of government.

No doubt this suggestion that the organs of participatory
democracy be given the authority to check one another in
order to avoid the formulation of excessively anti-producer or
anti-consumer policies will seem familiar to the attentive
reader. And so it should, for it constitutes the essence of the
political thought of Guild Socialism, especially of G. D. H.
Cole's *Guild Socialism Restated*. As will be remembered from
Chapter II, Cole asserted, for example, that milk prices for
a given area be set through negotiations between the relevant

dairy producers guild and representatives of the consumers cooperatives which purchased from that guild; and a guild in Cole's political philosophy is nothing but a body representative of the works councils of two or more factories (here milk processing plants) of a similar type. Likewise, he argued that questions of educational policy should be settled by negotiations between an Education Guild and a locally elected "Cultural Council."[33] (He also suggested something else very modish at present, i.e., that there should be provided "in every school the fullest facilities for self-government of the pupils."[34] He never did indicate, however, how the wishes of the bodies representing the parents and the teachers would be meshed with those of the student organization.) Substitute "teachers' works council" for "Educational Guild" and "neighborhood school board" for "Cultural Council," and you have one of the recommendations set forth in the above paragraphs, recommendations which we gladly admit are in fact based upon *Guild Socialism Restated*. In short, the Guild Socialist's version of participatory democracy was more realistic than that of most of the modern anti-bureaucratic socialists. Though Cole *said* that "there can be no real divergence of interest between [producers and consumers],"[35] it is clear that he thought that there *could* be: the demand that problems of concern to both groups be settled by negotiations between them assumes that, in the short run at least, what will benefit the producer will often hurt the consumer, and *vice versa*, even where profit making has been banned and both producer and consumer are represented by democratically elected organizations. As was earlier in this chapter, the modern anti-bureaucratic Left can justifiably be faulted for failing to perceive that this difference of interests might prevail in their participatory democracy; and certainly one of the intellectual problems it must wrestle with is how to bridge this gap.

There is one more vehicle not involving control from above which may be of use in making sure that the organs of participatory democracy that will be elected by *consumers* of goods and services will not be too anti-producer. If each neighborhood elected only one "legislature," and that body were to be made responsible for the performance of a wide variety of services (e.g., schools, local streets, welfare, police, fire, food and clothing stores), the chances are that among its constituents would be a considerable number of its employees. A community school board may have one or two of its teachers resident in the neighborhood but they would make up such a minute fraction of the community that the board would have little reason to pay much attention to their wishes. But were that school board transformed into a multi-purpose institution, the number of the "civil servants" it employed would multiply and so would the chances that a good number of these individuals would be inhabitants of the district. When this happened, the board might start worrying about trying to exploit any particular group among these civil servants. It would fear that an attack on teachers' wages would be construed by the policemen, firemen, etc. as the prelude to their own exploitation and consequently become alarmed that a step such as this would antagonize a not-inconsiderable percentage of its constituency. Such misgivings would, naturally, greatly reduce the chance that it would start abusing the teachers, welfare workers, etc.

So far, we have been talking about the various techniques that can be used to reduce the possibility of conduct by the organs of participatory democracy which many persons would label immoral: discriminating on racial or religious grounds, firing someone without giving him a chance to defend himself, taking a step (e.g., doubling the wages of one's constituents) which one knows or should know will severely threaten the welfare of others (e.g., the larger community and the consumer). But, as we have seen, there are possible adverse consequences of decentralist socialism which could not be said to be the "fault" of the local policy makers. It may lessen the chances of contact between the various ethnic groups of a pluralistic society and may result in a decrease in the quality of certain social services; but it would be unfair to attack a neighborhood school board for refusing to invite into its schools children from a neighboring community or for maintaining no German or French courses in its high school of three hundred or so. But even though we could not "blame" these local bodies in the event these consequences were to arise, it would nonetheless arguably be desirable if we could set up the new social system so as to prevent their occurrence. Actually, we have indicated earlier in this chapter how the increased separatism threatened by participatory democracy could be fought. Our weapon would once again be the higher levels of government, which could pass legislation requiring or "bribing" local school boards to accept some youngsters from other parts of town and, in turn, to send some of their children to school in different though not too distant communities. Similar measures could make it financially feasible for welfare agencies controlled by a Negro community to employ some whites, etc.

It is much more difficult to see how we would be able to increase the quality of the school, library, etc. systems operated by neighborhood groups. No community at present and for the next few decades will have the money to insure that every high school with five hundred or so children offers a wide variety of courses and that every neighborhood library system has one hundred thousand volumes plus subscriptions to all the major periodicals. We could, of course, extend the boundaries of the neighborhood school and library districts, but the advocates of participatory democracy would object that this would make it harder for the individual to be self-governing on educational, etc. issues. We could, instead, place high schools and libraries under city and even state control, but the same objection would be relevant. One possibility would be for the city to hire "roving" teachers of certain specialties for which there was some demand in most of the high schools but not enough in any one school to warrant its hiring a full-time teacher in that subject. These teachers could then spend part of the day in school A, part in school B, etc. Another step that could be taken is to extend the American "state library system" idea to the city by urging each "neighborhood library" system to specialize in a given field and requiring it to participate in a citywide library loan service. Or perhaps the city could maintain one large research library alongside of the numerous smaller neighborhood-controlled libraries. In any event, the advocates of participatory democracy should begin thinking of other solutions to these real problems.

To conclude this chapter, we must note that the Left would rightly insist that one important point has so far been totally ignored. We have been talking about *adverse* side-effects springing from the implementation of decentralist socialism; but we have failed to mention that it might produce certain *advantages* beyond a hoped-for increase in the number of self-governing citizens. What these extra benefits would be is obvious, but fairness demands that we mention them. (We shall defer to the last chapter our analysis of whether participatory democracy would in and of itself produce an increase in human brotherhood.)

Former United States Supreme Court Justice Louis D. Brandeis once defended the federal system of his country on the ground that it guaranteed the existence of forty eight (now fifty) laboratories for social experimentation. That is, thanks to American federalism, the United States is blessed with fifty political systems which can put into practice an idea for political or economic reform; and, moreover, the failure of a change adopted by just one or two of these systems will not hurt too many people or cost too much money. Now the numerous neighborhood legislatures that would come into being upon the widespread implementation of participatory democracy could be viewed as several thousand laboratories of the type Brandeis had in mind.[36] Thus a neighborhood school board in the United States might decide to adopt the "English" method of primary education; i.e., a scheme under which the children in a classroom are divided into groups, the teacher splits up his time among the groups and each group has a certain amount of freedom to do what it wishes. Now city-wide school boards in some of our big cities would probably be afraid at the present time to allow even one of their schools to try this approach to the education of small children. They (or those who appoint them) are responsible to a constituency whose majority is either satisfied with the *status quo* or wishes a return to even more "traditional" methods of learning than prevail now. But a local board elected by a sophisticated electorate (say the residents of Greenwich Village in New York City or of the Hyde Park area in Chicago) would feel that its electorate would be wholeheartedly in favor of this sort of experimentation or at least that it would be willing to give it a chance. Moreover, if an experiment such as this undertaken in one or two neighborhoods only would fail, so what! Its victims would be relatively few and there would still be plenty of "conventional" teachers who would be willing and able to remedy the harm which these children had suffered on account of having been exposed to the new method. Of course, if the new pedagogy should succeed, it would then probably be put into practice elsewhere as well.

To turn to the next "incidental" benefit that might spring from the adoption of participatory democracy, it could be argued that the new, smaller units of government would in certain respects be more efficient than the larger polities whose functions they would assume. This seems like an absurd contention for reasons noted earlier in this chapter. But there are a few ways in which the small institution *is* more efficient than the large. In the first place, every student of public administration contends that the top man in a department can only personally supervise between ten and twenty men. Thus the head of a welfare agency can personally check up upon all his social workers if the agency serves one neighborhood only but he certainly cannot do this if his agency has jurisdiction over an entire city. Also, the larger the institution the more paperwork it generally requires of its employees — and the thought of having to write out a good proposal in sextuplicate might deter an individual from making it in the first place. Moreover, when an organization grows too large its left hand might not know what its right hand is doing and consequently some of its employees may act in a way which unnecessarily duplicates or even contradicts the behavior of anothers. The catalogues of large universities are thus filled with redundant courses which involve a waste of scarce manpower; and one gets differing instructions about how to wrap a parcel for overseas mail each time he visits a different branch of the United States Post Office. Finally, in an institution of considerable size imaginative ideas are liable to get lost somewhere along the lengthy conveyor belt that connects the lowest level of the concern with the top.

To sum up, we have seen that participatory democracy may give rise to undesirable by-products even though it succeds in its goal of giving men more control over their lives. However, although any adventure has risks, there may be means of protecting ourselves from certain of these evils and, too, the new system may have some virtue beyond its ability to make men more self-governing. We have not as yet indicated whether these various considerations, when added to the evidence set forth in the prior chapters about whether it is likely in fact to have that particular consequence, demand that we accept or reject the views of the anti-statist radicals. In the concluding chapter, we shall balance against each other all these pros and cons, including a few more possible by-products of participatory democracy which we shall note there; but now let us make a detour to discuss one or two other matters.

FOOTNOTES TO CHAPTER VIII

1. Alan Altshuler's *Community Control* is a fervent and well-reasoned defense of the proposal to set up neighborhood governments. In his Chapter I he does mention most of the unfortunate side-effects we shall note (e.g. parochialism, anti-libertarianism, inefficiency, encouragement of racial separatism), though he believes neighborhood government is unlikely to promote them. However, his treatment of *why* neighborhood government may give rise to them is very different from ours. Chapter I of Cook and Morgan, *op. cit.* also touches upon most of the problems we shall discuss in this chapter.

2. What has appeared in this paragraph so far is based upon Neal, Fred. W., *Titoism in Action*, pp. 144-149 and *New York Times*, Jan. 9, 1962, p. 54.

3. "Yugoslavia Orders Control of Prices," *New York Times*, April 25, 1962, p. 7.

4. Underwood, Paul, "Red Regime Cuts Yugoslav Wages," *New York Times*, August 19, 1962, p. 13.

5. "Self Management with Tears," *The Economist*, February 24, 1968, p. 40.

6. Mayer, Martin, "The Full and Sometimes Very Surprising Story of Ocean Hill, the Teachers Union and the Teachers Strikes of 1968," *New York Times Magazine*, February 2, 1969, p. 18ff p. 20.

7. *Ibid.,* p. 42.

8. "Answering the Dissidents," *Civil Liberties in New York*, March 1969, p. 8. (Published by the New York Civil Liberties Union).

9. Mayer, *op. cit.*, p. 42.

10. "NYCLU In Ocean Hill," *Civil Liberties in New York*, March, 1969, p. 7.

11. "Answering the Dissidents," *Civil Liberties in New York*, March 1969, p. 8.

12. *Ibid.,* p. 58.

13. *Ibid.,* p. 58.

14. *Ibid.,* pp. 65-66.

15. See Chapter 4 of Lipset, Seymour, *op. cit.*

16. *Ibid.,* pp. 106-112.

17. *Ibid.,* p. 106.

18. Mayer, *op. cit.,* p. 64.

19. Lipset, *op. cit.,* pp. 87-79.

20. In connection with this discussion if the possibility of neighbor-
    hood organs of participatory democracy's hiring on an ethnic
    basis, we should note the very strange case of Dr. Arnold Ein-
    horn. Dr. Einhorn was chief of pediatrics at Lincoln Hospital,
    a city-run hospital in a poor Puerto Rican neighborhood in
    New York City. The Dean of the Medical School which staffed
    Lincoln removed him from this post, the relevant memoran-
    dum explicitly stating that it was necessary to have a director
    of a different ethnic background. Dr. Einhorn was Jewish as,
    ironically, was the Dean who ordered him removed. Einhorn had
    been the object of criticism by several community groups, as
    well as by the pediatricians working under him, and his succes-
    sor was a Puerto Rican. No one charged that Einhorn was an
    incompetent doctor; and one of the young doctors opposing
    him admitted that Einhorn was liked by the nurses and other
    hospital workers. This young doctor thought the reason for Dr.
    Einhorn's dismissal was not the fact that he was not Puerto
    Rican but that he had a rigid personality and thus that he
    could not get along well with his staff and his patients: the
    Dean himself orally denied after the memorandum had ben
    issued that the dischage had an ethnic basis (See New York
    Times Nov. 17, 1970 p. 1 and New York *Times* Nov. 18, 1970,
    p. 42). Whether the Dean's memorandum or his later oral
    statement contained the truth no one will ever know.

21. Carmichael, Stokely and Hamilton, Charles, *Black Power*
    (New York: Vintage Books, 1967), excerpted, p. 275, 276 of
    Cook and Morgan, *op. cit.*

22. This doctrine was used in e.g., *Hunter v. Erickson,* 393 U.S.
    358, (1969) in which the Supreme Court of the United States
    invalidated an amendment to the Akron city charter forbid-
    ding the implementation of "any ordinance dealing with
    racial, religious, or ancestral discrimination in housing without
    the approval of the majority of the voters." The Court's ra-
    tionale was that the amendment contained an explicitly racial
    classification.

23. 347 U.S. 483 (1954).

24. Mullen, Wm. F. — *Community Control and Black Political
    Participation,* at p. 256, 264 of Cook and Morgan, *op. cit.*

25. United States Commission on Civil Rights, *Racial Isolation in the Public Schools* (Washington, U.S. Government's Printing Office, 1967), at p. 113.

26. See p. 34 of his *Guild Socialism Restated* (London: Leonard Parsons, 1921).

27. See p. 282 of his *The Sane Society* (New York: Fawcett, 1965).

28. However, Cook and Morgan, scholars rather than advocates, are certainly aware of the possibility of such a conflict, See *op. cit.*, p. 39. The same is true, on a subconscious level, for those who want the university governed by committees representing students, administration, and faculty.

29. See p. 85 of his *Southern Legacy* (Baton Rouge: Louisiana State University Press, 1950).

30. Altshuler suggests (*op. cit.*, p. 155) that employees of neighborhood governments should be protected by "state standards with regard to probationary periods and safeguards against arbitrary dismissal of tenured employees."

31. Cook and Morgan say (*op. cit.*, p. 38) that many units of neighborhood government will require financial aid from above.

32. According to Cook and Morgan, *Ibid.*, p. 38, "One can imagine jurisdictional disputes and other quarrels that beset contemporary state and local political institutions cropping up just as frequently among these new units."

33. Cole, *op. cit.*, Chapter VI.

34. *Ibid.*, p. 111.

35. *Ibid.*, p. 29.

36. Paul Goodman, in his *People or Personnel* (New York: Random House, 1963), excerpted, p. 49, 51 of Cook and Morgan, *op. cit.*, notes that decentralization in education would lead to more experimentation.

IX

WHY THE DEMAND
FOR PARTICIPATORY DEMOCRACY?

The problem of why it is the late 1960's and early 1970's that are seeing the rebirth of the demand for the establishment of a decentralized socialism is a intriguing one for the social scientist, whether he be historian, political scientist, anthropologist, psychologist or economist. Superficially, it is a very easy matter to solve. All that we have to do, many would argue, is look to the conditions under which some of the groups calling for decentralist socialism are living and you have your answer. There are the students subjected to tremendous pressure all through high school, grammar school or lycée just so they will be able to get into a college of their (for which read "their parents' ") choice. Then, when they arrive in this "utopia," what do they find? They are afflicted by huge lecture sessions probably taught (at least in the United States) by a graduate assistant who is mainly interested in getting his doctoral dissertation out of the way; by graduation requirements which seem to them absurd; by a choice of courses which is framed entirely by the faculty; by professors who are too busy worrying about their next book or article to have anything to do with them; and by a system of required exams, papers and grades. No wonder they demand "student power." Likewise, the American Negro is the victim of abuses which are too well known to have to catalogue here; and it thus is no surprise that he demands the creation of a social system under which he can control his own fate. The American anti-bureaucratic radicals and their European analogues are composed of students or ex-students who have, in addition, been made aware by teachers, parents and television of the plight of exploited people in their own country and in other parts of the world; and their "liberal" parents have said that something ought to be done about these wrongs (while doing nothing about them themselves). Thus it is not surprising that they call out for student power, black power, workers' power, etc. And the French Canadians, Welsh and Scots separatists, etc. feel that their ethnic groups are being discriminated against, which indicates the popularity of "Long Live Free Quebec," etc. (Since the explanation for the rise of anti-bureaucratic radicalism at this period of history applies also to the regional separatism which is rampant today, since the far left in these regions is mainly separatist, too, and since both regional separatism and participatory democracy favor transferring power from the larger to the smaller, we shall treat both these phenomena together in this Chapter even though there is obviously a real distinction between the region on the one hand and the neighborhood or factory on the other.)

But this will not do as an adequate analysis of why there is so much more talk of decentralist socialism now than formerly. Students have been oppressed by smaller conditions for a hundred years; American Negroes have led a miserable existence ever since they were dragged to the new world; Quebec has never been independent; and the days of Welsh and Scottish freedom have long since ended. Yet students have rarely, during the previous century, demanded a substantial say in academic matters; the American Negro community produced no major separatist movements after the decline of Garveyism's call for "back to Africa" in the early 1920's; the demand for the end of the Anglo-French-Canadian union was rather muffled until now; and, e.g., Scotland made no significant demand for more autonomy after the romantic days of Bonnie Prince Charlie in 1745. In fact, both Wales and Scotland were strongholds of the Labor Party. So a recital of the actual or felt plight of the Scots, Welsh, students, Negroes, etc. only starts us on the road to a real understanding of why the demand for decentralist socialism is more widespread now than it used to be. Obviously if, e.g., the American Negro as a group thought that it had no problems, no one would ever utter the cry of "black power;" but during the 1940's, 50's, and early 60's his sea of troubles was deep but he and the American left as a whole (except for the Communist Party) were much more interested in integration than in voluntary *apartheid*.

Nor will a discussion of the failings of American and European capitalism get us too for. Naturally, if the capitalist countries had eliminated poverty, had not been plagued by race prejudice, and had eschewed military operations in areas of the world inhabited by non-whites, the left would not at present have been urging that capitalism be dismantled. But once again, the English and French empires, hunger in big city and rural slums, and American billion dollar expenditures on defense only explain the call for "socialism," — and not why "decentralism" is considered as the proper form of socialism. One hears capitalism attacked as a wasteful, inefficient system and yet the anti-bureaucratic radical pleads for workers' control of industry rather than the implementation of a national economic plan. And the weaknesses of capitalism do not provide us with the reasons why this preference is currently in vogue! All the groups now demanding the creation of small-scale institutions which the average man can control have had real or imaginary grievances and been aware of capitalism's flaws for quite a while. Accordingly, we cannot explain this demand simply by pointing to these grievances and flaws, especially as in the past these groups turned to orthodox socialism or other remedies for their respective predicaments.

Jack Newfield has contended that

> the New Radicalism is an existential revolt against
> remote, impersonal machines that are not responsive to
> human needs. The New Radicals feel sharply the grow-
> ing totalitarianization of life in this technological, urban
> decade. They feel powerless and unreal beneath the un-
> feeling instruments that control their lives . . . The
> New Radicals are the first products of liberal affluence
> . . . They are the children of economic surplus and
> spiritual starvation.[1]

Compressed into these several sentences is a thesis that forms
much of the crux of this Chapter, the proposition that decentralist socialism is attracting adherents now because of the
greater remoteness of the decision-makers who determine the
fate of the ordinary citizen, because of the real prosperity of
our age, and because human reason has been used to achieve
aims that appear perverted to many people. Let us turn to
these points in detail.

Point one is that there is more stress now on decentralist
socialism partly because most vital policy decisions are and
appear to be made at a new level that is further from the
average man than was the old; and because it is now fairly
clear that the newer level — or one yet more distant — will
be the crucial one in the future unless something drastic
is done about the situation. To begin with, the Port Huron
Statement of the Students for a Democratic Society refers to
"the very isolation of the individual from power . . . ," and
to the "structural remoteness" of "the great mass of people
. . . with respect to democratic institutions. . . "[2] Mario Savio,
one of the leaders of the "Free Speech" protests at the University of California at Berkeley in 1964, notes that "In our
free speech fight at the University of California, we have
come up against what may emerge as the greatest problem of
our nation — depersonalized, unresponsive bureaucracy . . .
Here we find it impossible usually to meet anyone but secre-
taries. Beyond that, we find functionaries who cannot make

policy but can only hide behind the rules."[3] So there is certainly a feeling among some of the best-known participatory democrats that whoever makes the crucial decisions these days is hard for the average man — i.e., you and I, Savio and Kafka's Mr. K. — to reach, to contact, to influence one way or the other. But this does not yet fully prove our point, for we have not yet shown that this "whoever" is further removed from the mass of men than his counterpart in prior years. Unless we can demonstrate this, we have not said much about what it is now until now that much of the left has begun emphasizing decentralization. (If "he" had been as removed then as "he" is now, a theory that "his" distance is one cause of today's call for decentralist socialism would be a weak one.)

The evidence we have to back up this hypothesis that makers of crucial decisions are now more distant than before is extensive. It consists, to a large extent, of the obvious point that the central government in almost every nation has in fact now much more power over the individual and groups than it had in the past. In the United States, as late as the early decades of this century it was his employer plus perhaps state and local governments which made the decisions which significantly affected the way in which the average man lived. Whether one kept his job depended mainly on the whim of the employer; and if he was fired his only recourse was to the poor relief provided by the municipality. The quality of education he received and what happened to him after he left school was once again up to those to whom he applied for a job and to the local government which could grant him a pittance as a "dole." We are not arguing that in, e.g., 1905 the individual was in much more control of his life than he is now; but merely that the people who in fact determined his fate were individuals he could speak to personally and institutions whose members he could contact fairly easily.

But look what happens to him today. Whether he gets a

good or poor education depends in part on how much money the federal government decides to pour into his school district. Between eighteen and twenty-six he lives under the threat of being forced by the government to spend two years in the armed forces, at best a boring existence and at worst a highly dangerous one which may get one killed fighting for a cause about which he is extremely sceptical. Then he leaves the service and applies for a job. The chances are good that if he applies to a private employer it will be one which performs "defense-related contracts," and which thus would be likely to fire him were aid from Uncle Sam to cease to be forthcoming. Even if he applies for a state or city job, he may well find that the agency for which he works is partly financed by Washington. Of course, if he is discharged he will receive unemployment compensation for six months — and state unemployment compensation schemes exist only because federal legislation makes it politically possible for states to enact them. After six months expire, his family will receive funds under the federally financed AFDCU program — if he lives in one of the states which have introduced it. The length of time he must wait to get a new position depends on the buoyancy of the economy, and this in turn depends a great deal upon the extent and direction of federal spending and upon a decision of the Federal Reserve Board to facilitate the extension of credit by private banks. The amount of renumeration he receives in his new post is very likely to be affected by federal statutes setting minimum wages and permitting workers to organize into unions and bargain collectively. Finally, it cames time for this man to retire. To a large extent he and his spouse will keep alive thanks to a social security check issued him by the national government, checks which his wife will continue to receive even after he dies. We do not contend that the hypothetical individual we have been discussing will be fully conscious of the extent to which he is dependent upon the policites of the national government; but the chances are that he will have some insight into his real situation and thus feel himself more its ward than did his father's father who died in 1920.

Not only has the control over the fate of the average man shifted in great part from the local and regional to the national level over the past forty or fifty years, but, moreover, the non-national institutions with which he deals have become more sizeable or remote. The chances are that the company he works for is a lot bigger than it was when grandfather was employed there and that his university is two or three times as large as it was in even his father's day. His grandfather may well have been a farmer or a resident of a small town: he is more likely to be a resident of a big city. Even if he lives in a suburb, the quality of his life hangs upon decision made by important persons in the central city (e.g., about whether or not to make the center of town a more pleasant place to visit, to improve the network of commuter railroads connecting the city and the suburbs, to pass an air pollution law). As a result of all this, he is less likely than his grandfather to be able to personally contact the men who set the policy that regulates his job, the deans and professors who fashion the pattern of his college career, and the local politicians and businessmen whose resolutions can determine whether or not the area in which he lives smacks more of Jersey City, New Jersey than of San Francisco, California. And for these reasons, too, he is more likely than his grandfather to perceive that the persons controlling his life are far-away figures whom he has no chance at all to influence.

Applying this general analysis to the particular groups that are at present in the forefront of the fight for decentralist socialism, we find that it is surely applicable to today's college students. Continuing to limit ourselves for a while to the United States, we find that the draft, the big university, the possibility of obtaining a scholarship, loan, or research grant from Washington are all conducive to making him feel more dependent than the student of 1910 or 1925 upon distant power centers. As for the members of left-wing groups such as the Students for a Democratic Society, these are mainly students or ex-students and the factors just mentioned have thus touched their lives as well. On the other hand, the radical groups that flourished at the start of the century were made up to a considerable extent of employees of relatively small firms — e.g., sweatshops, mines, manufacturing concerns with ten to twenty employees, etc. "The boss" may have been a greedy exploiter — but at least he was around. The fate of the American Negro after the federal troops were withdrawn from the south in 1876 remained almost exclusively in the hands of state politicians and local whites until the national government started taking some interest in his problems once again. This can be said to have occurred in the 1940's, when President Harry Truman by executive order ended racial discrimination in the United States Army and the United States Supreme Court held (a) that state courts could not enforce agreements by neighbors not to sell to colored people[4] and (b) that a political party could not exclude blacks from its primary elections.[5] Since then, of course, the federal government has promulgated a torrent of policy of great interest to the Negro, including not only bills and court cases banning racial discrimination but spending programs such as the Economic Opportunity Act of 1964 and the broad Elementary and Secondary Education Act of 1965. Finally, Canada, Britain and France, three countries where left wing regional separatist movements have been powerful recently, have witnessed in recent years even more of a shift of power from the private, local and procincial levels to the national. In Canada, for example, the Dominion Government is now active in the fields of medical care, unemployment compensation, old age and survivors insurance and farm pricee supports. And everyone knows the great expansion in the activities of the British central government that was the harvest of the Labor administration of 1945-51. Coal, electricity, gas, steel and the railroads have been nationalized; the state operates a comprehensive program of medical insurance that allows everyone in the country to have medical care at minimal expense; the government can now declare that a particular price or wage boost is illegal; a quarter of the British people live in housing it financed, etc. Decisions vitally affecting the student, the American Negro, the members of radical groups, and the residents of regions clearly distinct from the rest of the country are and appear to be promulgated by men more removed geographically, with larger constituencies, and having more employees who serve as buffers between them and the people than those who made similar decisions at the turn of this century.

The attentive reader will no doubt retort that this does not yet show why the political thought of these groups is of a decentralist variety. It is true, he would say, that central governments have become busier, that employer have become bigger, etc. But it is not self-evident that the groups we have cited should be concerned about this particular fact. On the whole, the bigger, more remote policy-maker is a juster master than were the local, private and/or diminutive lords of men's fate sixty or seventy years ago. Uncle Sam drafts the students; but it also gives him the fellowship that his city or state refused to give to his father or grandfather. It sends federal officials to the south to assure that the Negro will be able to vote while fifty or so years ago southern state and county legislators spent their time conjuring up ingenious devices designed to make certain that he would *not* be able to cast a ballot. The Welsh miner of today is treated much more gingerly by his public employer, the National Coal Board, than his father was by the small private company that ran the local mine with a maximum of inattention to the safety and health of its workers. And the British government is a lot surer to pay his medical bills than were his relatives.

It is probably true that, both in respect to the groups we are considering specially and to the ordinary people generally, today's "distant" decision-makers are much more merciful and much more helpful than were the "just on the other side of the tracks" power-elites of the early 1900's. Even the heads of the large multiversities are more tolerant of political and religious unorthodoxy and less overly-protective of their co-eds than were the presidents of these institutions when they were mere colleges or universities. But in practice people do worry about the fact that the locus of decision-making has moved further and further from their grasp even at the same time that they applaud the actions of the new decision-makers. Whether this worry is logically consistent or not is beyond the scope of this book: what is important for our purposes is the fact that it does exist. Gabriel Almond and Sidney Verba have shown that most people in the United States believe that their national government "improves conditions" when it acts.[6] Yet Duane Lockard indicates that a good number of American citizens fear that this century's increases in federal power will lead to the destruction of the American democracy[7] The Swedish economist Gunnar Myrdal is wholeheartedly in favor of the welfare state, but complains that its implementation at present relies too much on direct state intervention as opposed to popular participation.[8] Walter Heller was one of the most important advisers to the liberal Democratic Kennedy and Johnson administrations in the United States and favored strong action by the federal government to insure full employment, price stability, and rapid economic growth. However, at the same time, he demands the revitalization of state governments through the use of revenue sharing: i.e., grants of money by the federal government to the states to spend more or less as they like. And one of his arguments for the revitalization of the states, i.e., that state and local governments are the vehicles of the dispersion of power necessary to the preservation of democracy, shows that he, too, feels queasy about the result of the increased national activity he himself demands.[9]

To recapitulate, contrary to what might appear to be the

case on first glance, the mere fact that the central government is more benevolent than private employers or local politicians does not always mean that one will be happy that an inaccessible institution has taken over functions formerly performed less satisfactorily by a nearby one. And one who is uncomfortable about this will be desirous or further restructuring society in such a way as to retain the benefits of the transfer of these activities while at the same time nullifying the allegedly distressing effects of the switch. For example, Charles Hamilton, one of the most articulate exponents of the doctrines that blacks should conrol black communities, has written that "Some Black Power advocates are aware that this country is experiencing centralization and decentralization. As the Federal Government becomes more involved (and it must) in the lives of people, it is imperative that we broaden the base of citizen participation."[10] Most of the decentralist socialists would disagree with Dr. Hamilton that the federal government must become *more* involved in the lives of people, but the majority would confess that the "decentralism" in their political thought is a reaction against the fact that it has become so involved already!

Two more points must be mentioned before leaving this question of the relationship between an increase in the remoteness of the crucial decision makers and the growth in popularity of "decentralist socialism." The migration of decision-making from local and regional governments and small or medium sized private firms to the national government and large business and educational enterprises can be said to have started on a large scale during the 1930's. This was the decade in which the Great Depression of 1929 and succeeding years forced the governments in the western world to take a more active role in economic affairs. And during the 1940's, as a result of World War II and of socialist participation in the governments of France and Britain, this particular trend was accelerated. Why, then, if decentralist socialism is in part a product of this change in the nature or the identity of the important decision-makers, did it not, after its "death" in the 1920's become popular again before the 1960's? First, the switch to decentralist socialism is a reaction, arising from a perception of centralization, and often a phenomenon occurs before people become fully cognizant of it. Also, it was not apparent that centralization would be a *permanent* feature of western politico-economic systems until the War had been over a few years. Thirdly, the energies involved in winning the war prevented left-wing theorists from thinking about alternatives to the centralized socialism that was then in vogue. Fourth, because of the Soviet Union's contribution to the Allied effort, a few of these theorists forgot their anger at Stalin's purge trials and the Hitler-Stalin pact and once again became intrigued by the Soviet experiment in centralized socialism.[11] Fifth, the Labour government in post-war England and the Socialists who participated in the revolving cabinets of post-war France were faced with the gargantuan task of reviving ravaged economies which had to be rebuilt to a level at which these nations could compete successfully in the world market. These socialists were, therefore, afraid to take any step (such as the establishment of factory works councils with real power) which might make their countries' industrial systems less efficient. Finally, in the United States during the heydey of McCarthyism (1950-55), many people hesitated to espouse *any* form of socialism; and it is probable that throughout the West a significant number of individuals refused to even think about the desirability of socialism of any sort just because the overtly totalitarian Stalinist regime in Russia happened to apply the label of "socialist" to itself. (One might think that the revelation by Khruschev of Stalin's terror and the 1956 Russian suppression of the Hungarian revolution would have been important factors in turning socialists away from centralization. However, two writers who have studied the SDS movement contend that though the young radicals of the early 1960's "refused to identify with the Soviet Union," they were not "greatly concerned about injustice in any of the Communist societies."[12])

That decentralist socialism is to some extent a consequence of an apparent increase in the distance between people and decision maker is confirmed by yet another consideration. As we saw in an earlier chapter, the first decade of the twentieth century were filled with decentralist socialist ideas — the Guild Socialist movement in England was born then and the French Syndicalists were popular. And this decade marked the end of another era in which those who formulated important policy had become more inaccessible to those who were affected by that policy. Especially on the continent and in the United States the last decades of the old century had been marked by a growth in the size of private business enterprises. The national governments in countries such as Germany had assumed more responsibility for economic affairs and for the welfare of the inhabitants of their nation; and some of the British Guild Socialists were left wingers who were terrified by the fact that it was the government at *Westminster* which sought in 1910 to enact schemes of health and unemployment insurance. And these governments headed nations that had, in one way or another, become much larger during the past forty or so years. A region consisting of Prussia plus a whole host of little cities and principalities had developed into a single and powerful nation-state. And though Britain and France had not officially enlarged their borders, they had during this period seized for themselves numerous colonies in Africa and Asia. The British government was transformed from a ruler of forty million into a master of hundreds of millions: and one can assume that the forty million felt that members of "their" government thus had even less time for them individually than they did before.

The second major reason for the increased emphasis on decentralization among socialists is a rather paradoxical one: the increase in the material prosperity of the western world. This is, of course, a frequently mentioned cause of student activism: young men and women who have been brought up in a home overflowing with material goods but empty of happiness are bound to react against a society which emphasizes as the *summum bonum* the acquisition of new cars, refrigerators and devices for making one more sexually attractive. Likewise, because of economic expansion, these young people are more or less assured of some job upon graduation regardless of how well they have done academically and thus can devote time to radical causes without worrying too much about how this will affect them later.[13] Then, of course, fewer need jobs while at college and thus more have time for politics. But this oft-heard explanation of student activism does not fully show the connection between prosperity and the call for participatory democracy. (Why, for example, have not the great majority of new student activists made "centralized socialism" their rallying cry?)

Prosperity has made the current left more favorably inclined toward decentralization because, first of all, it makes less obvious the need for an immediate increase in the activities of the national activities which in all likelihood be carried on by it directly or by local or regional governments under policies which it sets. As Charles Frankel has said, "The welfare state is a postcript to emergency, the heritage that has been left with us by the disasters of depression and war."[14] We are not, of course, asserting that in times of boom the sphere of activity of the central government will *never* increase. In the United States, as we saw, it passed all sorts of social legislation during the prosperous years of Lyndon B. Johnson's administration: economic recession is not the only cause of the expansion of the powers of the nation state. All that we are arguing is that when thousands or millions of people are starving, the liberal or socialist is *most* likely to demand massive expenditure by the state upon public works and relief and the nationalization of large enterprises so that they can be kept open and thus continue to employ people even though they no longer realize an immediate monetary profit.[15] In a depression such as the one afflicting the western world during the 1930's, the rapid expansion of the powers and operations of the central political system seem to the radical the only sensible way of averting large scale disaster. But when people are prosperous, or at least when no one is in danger of starving, then the man or woman who wishes to transform society can in good conscience propose models for reform that seem less threatening to the individual. Control of industry by factory works councils rather than by the state with the resultant possibility of rather high prices for consumers' goods seems sheer suicide when large numbers of people have no money to buy food. But where people are so affluent that they all will have enough to purchase at least the necessities of life, it ceases to be absurd to demand experimentation with workers' control of industry. Likewise, when the nation is wealthy it becomes less impractical to abandon large-scale public works in favor of unconditional grants to community legislatures for use in relieving poverty and unemployment in less tried-and-true and thus more-likely-to-fail ways. Similarly, when a region such as Wales is plagued with poverty and unemployment, Welshmen would laugh at the suggestion that the area cut its ties to the rest of Britain. For an absolutely impoverished area of wild mountains, coal mines and digny industrial towns to take a step which would mean the end of a subsidy from its relatively wealthy cousin would strike everyone as ludicrous, especially where the more favored relative could hardly be said to be a tyrant. However, let the fear of starvation vanish from the hills and glens and then their residents will be much more receptive to the idea of independence. (For "Wales" in the above sentences the reader should feel free to insert "Quebec," "Brittany," and/or "Scotland.")

The fact that the American Negro is demanding political and economic decentralization also shows that prosperity is an important cause of the demand for control by a community of its own institutions. Though the Negro is third from the bottom when it comes to ranking American ethnic groups in the order of material well being — only Mexican Americans and American Indians do worse — and though the disparity between his economic position and that of the whites has slightly increased over the past twenty or so years, he is better off in an absolute sense than he was two decades ago. For example, in 1947 only seven percent of Negro families earned over $7,000; in 1966 the percentage was twenty-eight. And in the former year sixty-five of all American Negro families earned less than $3,000, while in 1966 the corresponding figure was down to thirty-two percent.[16] The progress has been real, and has continued since 1966, even when one takes into account inflation during these years. Furthermore, he is more "prosperous" in a non-material sense. Even in the American south, he no longer lives under the constant fear of sudden and irrational white violence that plagued him in the 1920's; and he has in fact obtained the basic political right of voting. For the first time since his arrival in the western hemisphere, as the above considerations show, the average Negro is free from the worry of figuring out how he and his family will be able to physically survive until the morrow. This means that he has the time and peace of mind to think about the various ways in which he has been told that he can improve his condition even more and to then pick and choose among these several alternatives. And one of these options which he now has the physical leisure and mental energy to contemplate is "black power," i.e., black control of institutions in Negro areas. (Incidentally, if the above paragraphs are true, a continuation of the "Nixon-Heath" recession of '70-'72 will mean a temporary diminution of the call for decentralist socialism.)

One more significant reason for the recent turn to "decentralist" socialism is that the left seems to be reacting against rationality. In a sense, participatory democracy is, as we have seen, an "irrational" system. It is irrational not in the sense that its implementation would *necessarily* produce inefficiency; but only in the sense that putting it into practice would make it *less likely* that certain functions would be carried out with a reasonable degree of efficiency. To repeat some points we have previously made: the services which a neighborhood political unit would furnish might not be able to take advantage of economies of size; and consequently these services might either be inadequate or very expensive per capita. Moreover, decentralist socialism would make it more probable that new investment would not flow into areas where it was most needed. For example, were workers to have absolute control over their factories, there would be nothing to prevent them from concentrating too greatly on the production of consumers goods which are temporarily in great demand and thus to neglect the production of the capital goods which must be fabricated if the economy is to be healthy in the future. Likewise, there would be nothing to prevent several firms from simultaneously deciding to produce one particular commodity, e.g., cars, a state of affairs which would soon produce an excess of automobiles and a shortage of, e.g., washing machines. A socialist who placed the highest emphasis upon rationality would probably favor an economy and a political system in which the producers of goods and services could have a big market for their products — so that they could profit by economies of size; and in which they were subject to rather stringent coordination at the national or at least the regional level so that the curse of wasted investment could be eradicated. Only such a system, at least at present, would insure a good quantity of high quality goods and services at reasonable cost.

Why should many modern socialists prefer irrationality to rationality? Primarily, it seems, because many of our current woes are traceable in part to certain misuses of human brain power. Human reason, including both deductive and inductive thinking, is potentially the salvation of the world. However, in the words of Herbert Marcuse, "The scientific method which led to the ever-more-effective domination of nature thus came to provide the pure concepts as well as the instrumentalities for the ever-more-effective domination of man by man through the domination of nature."[17]

To make several points in explication of Marcuse's position, the whole arsenal of modern armaments, with its power to infect the race with dread disease and to destroy every living thing on earth, is a product of several sorts of thinking. It results, in the first place, from the use of deductive reasoning, almost always using premises which are formulated quantitatively, to discover the laws governing the physical universe. The engineer then engages in more deductive reasoning to discover how these laws can be used in a specific situation to satisfy certain ends posited by the state, e.g., the defoliation of jungles which conceal the guerillas against whom the military is warring at the moment. Both the general propositions and their practical end-products are then subject to what we can call empirical reasoning. The propositions are tested in the laboratory to determine whether they can be directly or indirectly confimed by observation while the results are tested on army proving grounds and (sometimes) on yellow or brown skinned civilians to see whether they "work."[18] Of course, not only our armament cache, but our entire economic system as well, is the product of a fusion of empirical and deductive reasoning. And as a result of this economic system the air and waters are polluted, the countryside is dotted with jerry-built, look-alike houses, hours are spent stalled in traffic jams, and millions face unemployment due to automation. There is a third type of reasoning, which can be analyzed into a combination of empirical and deductive reasoning but which we can consider separately here, which in the opinion of many has had peculiarly inhumane results in recent years. This is what its most famous exponent calls "systems analysis."[19] It postulates that we (usually the nation) have a particular opponent and that it is good to destroy him or at least remain independent of him, and will then explore in an intellectually sophisticated manner the various alternatives for victory or survival open to "us" when "we" and "they" are in a certain position. It is by the use of this sort of reasoning that we have developed various strategies for determining how we can kill ninety percent of the population of the Soviet Union without having them destroy more than fifty percent of ours.

Many who feel that human reason is being abused in all these ways react. Some, of course, employ force or the threat of force against their real or imagined opponents rather than by persuading them through cogent arguments. The physical expulsion of some deans from a building at Harvard by the SDS in spring, 1969, and the forcible removal of some visiting parents from the union building at Cornell the same semester are some of the more obvious examples of these tactics. Some of course, hit out against the cultural tradition which their teachers seek to impart to them. The widely-held belief among the radical students and blacks that history is irrelevant and that good spelling and grammar are totally useless typify this aspect of the rebellion. And, most importantly for our purposes, many of them propose a social order which left-wing systems analysts would reject simply because it might well make more difficult the accomplishment of some of the important goals of decentralist socialism itself, especially that of the abolition of poverty. The antistatist radicals see the human brain as the producer of Hiroshima, Auschwitz, Vietnam and air pollution and thus call for the establishment of a social system which is, on the surface at least, more appealing to the heart than to the mind. Of course it is not mind itself but mind profaned that has given rise to these evils; but the distinction has been forgotten in the need for quick action to end them!

To continue with this discussion of why decentralist socialism is so popular now with the left, we must take notice of a phenomenon that, we may call a "dialectic of ideas," (a bit different in form from the Hegelian thesis-antithesis-

synthesis). There seems to be tendency in the realm of ideology for one idea to be popular with a certain group for a
while; then to be replaced in its affections by a way of looking at things that seems quite different; and then to be re-
turned to its former position of prominence, perhaps though
not always slightly modified in the light of the requirements
of the "opposed" view which is losing its place in the sun.
For example, in the area of literary criticism, it was once the
fashion to concentrate upon the social and historical background of a novel, poem or drama. Then along came the
"new critics," who contended that to understand a work of
literature one must not go beyond its "four corners". At present, however, the new critics seem to admit that full com-
prehension can come only after a study of the relevant bio-
graphical and sociological data as well as of the words, techniques and style of the author. In the historical sphere, the
idea of the equality of men was in the forefront during the
end of the eighteenth century and the beginning of the nineteenth. Then during the latter portion of the nineteenth
and the first four and one half decades of the twentieth it
was eclipsed by the idea that one race was better than another, more specifically that the white race was superior to
the brown and yellow races and that northern European
whites made up the world's best racial stock. At present
most persons pay at least lip-service to the idea of equality,
which now (unlike that defended by Thomas Jefferson in
the eighteenth century), includes the black man as well.

Similarly, the idea of "decentralist socialism" appears to
be subject to this dialectic of ideas. As noted previously, it
was fashionable during the first half of the nineteenth century. It enjoyed a revival beginning with the end of that
century but was tossed aside during the 1920's in favor of a
more centralist vision of public control of the economy. And
its recrudescence in the 1960's is in part attributable to this
tendency for people to turn a view that seems dissimilar to
that which they had previously espoused. The idea of de-

centralist socialism is discarded in favor of that of orthodox socialism — and this is in turn later elbowed aside by the theory of decentralist socialism which is now called back from exile!

Why many ideas are subject to such a dialectic can probably be more easily clarified by the psychologist than by the sociologist. I would presume that one reason for the "dialectical behavior" of schools of thought is that the human mind is creative and is thus bound to be discontent with the theses that presently prevail. (As many of these theses are flawed or will lead to tragedy in practice, the dialectic is a necessary instrument of human progress, though its effects can be destructive — as witnessed by the replacement a hundred years ago of the idea of human brotherhood by the idea of racial superiority.) On a more cynical plane, one can assume that another reason for this ebb and flow of ideas is that certain individuals want attention and fame. One sure way of getting this is to put one's weight behind a doctrine different from that generally accepted; though the idea must not be too different or unpopularity rather than prestige will ensue.

Of course, we must add several major caveats to the views enunciated in the three previous paragraphs. Most importantly, we are not claiming that all ideas are subject to this dialectic; but merely that there is a good chance that an idea will dance to its tune, that there is a *tendency* for ideas to wax and wane in popularity in a dialectical pattern. There are many times when the decline of an idea seems irreversible, where "progress" travels along a straight line. In classical music, for example, harmony was replaced by dissonance in the early part of this century; and much music that is currently being written by serious composers is even more atonal. In the novel the realism of Balzac, France and Dreiser is still being replaced by one of several alternative techniques, — the stream of consciousness of a Joyce, the turgidity of a Faulkner, the fantasy of a Tolkien or Barth, and the allegory of a Golding. Also the dialectic we are discussing is one in the realm of the intellect only, and is not always reflected in the real world. Though most people reject the accusation that they are racists and believe sincerity in the idea of human brotherhood, racism is a noose which is threatening to asphyxiate many of the major nations of the earth. Likewise, though decentralist socialism is popular today, governments that label themselves socialist are committed in practice and usually in theory to centralist socialism. Finally, that an idea waxes and wanes in popularity, does not mean that no one adheres to its opposite during the period when it is "in" and that everyone rejects it during the eras when its opposite is "chic." Some good writers of the present day (e.g., Philip Roth) do not hesitate to adopt the technique of literary realism, even though this style may never regain its popularity with the literary *cognoscenti*. And there are, as we have just indicated, many socialists who are still committed to a centralized version of socialism, just as men such as G. D. H. Cole always argued for a form of decentralism even during the years when many on the far left were entranced by the successes of the "centralistic" five-year plans of the Soviet Union.

FOOTNOTES TO CHAPTER IX

1. Newfield, Jack, *A Prophetic Minority*, (New York: Ne wAmerican Library, 1966), p. 23.
2. Jacobs and Landau (ed.), *The New Radicals*, p. 160.
3. *Ibid.*, pp. 230-231.
4. *Shelley v. Kraemer*, 334 U.S. 1 (1948).
5. *Smith v. Allwright*, 321 U.S. 649 (1944).
6. Almond, Gabriel and Verba, Sidney, *The Civic Culture* (Princeton: Princeton University Press, 1963) p. 82.
7. Lockard, Duane, *Governing the State and Localities*, 2nd ed. (New York: Macmillan, 1969), p. 32.
8. Myrdal, Gunnar, *Beyond the Welfare State* (New York: Bantam Books, 1971) p. 82-83.
9. Heller, Walter, *New Dimensions of Political Economy* (Cam-

bridge: Harvard University Press, 1966), pp. 58-60, 125, 147.

10. See his "An Advocate of Black Power Defines It," New York *Times Magazine,* April 14, 1968, p. 22 at p. 83.

11. See, e.g., G. D. H. Cole, The Intelligent Man's Guide to the Post-War World (London: Gollancz, 1957), pp. 797-802. Though Cole said that he was "tempermentally antagonistic" to Stalin (p. 798), he added that (p. 799) "As far as I am able to see, the internal policy of the Soviet Union has been consistently directed in the interests of the main body of the people and has aimed, first at consolidating and securing the victory of the Revolution, and secondly, at raising standards of productivity with a view to advancing the standards of living as far and as fast as this can be done consistently with the first object."

12. Jacobs and Landau, *op. cit.,* p. 12.

13. One can continue to make this point, even though there is now (1972) a job shortage for college graduates, because the development of campus radicalism took place in the sixties, a period when there were plenty of positions for them.

14. Frankel, Charles, *The Democratic Prospect* (New York: Harper and Row, 1962), Chapter I, at p. 207 of Schottland, Chas. (ed.) *The Welfare State* (New York: Harper & Row, 1967)

15. It could be argued that some of the reforms of the Johnson administration (e.g., medicare) were the result of initiatives from people living under emergency conditions (e.g., the aged).

16. See the *Report of the National Advisory Commission on Civil Disorders* (The Kerner Commission) (New York: Bantam Books, 1968), at p. 250.

17. See Marcuse, Herbert, *One Dimensional Man* (Boston: Beacon Paperbacks, 1966), p. 158.

18. Incredible as it may seem, Seymour M. Hersh reports at p. 149 of his *Chemical and Biological Warfare: America's Hidden Arsenal* (Indianapolis: Bobbs-Merrill, 1968), that "in mid-1967, another high-level Pentagon official told me that three factors led to the decision to use defoliants in Vietnam.

    1. The need to conduct defoliation experiments in heavy jungle areas. . . . "

19. Kahn, Herman, *On Thermonuclear War* (Princeton: Princeton University Press, 1961), p. viii.

X

PARTICIPATORY DEMOCRACY, YES OR NO?

We have spent a great deal of time giving the reader the many pros and cons of decentralist socialism. As with most proposed reforms, this one has its merits and demerits, its potential strengths and its potential failings. But to say this is obviously not enough. As men and women, we are all faced with the duty of choice. We shall be less than truly human if we simply evade a decision for or against the *status quo*. And, if we opt for change, we are then faced, at the very least, with having to analyze whether a suggested alternative to the present scheme of things is best. On the assumption, therefore, that the present-day modified capitalist welfare state is outmoded on economic and/or moral grounds; and that the very existence of a large "private" economic sector prevents modern technology from being employed to its fullest extent, accustoms people to acting from selfish motives, and makes them incapable of acting to alleviate the misery of the lowest groups on the social totem pole; we must decide whether decentralist socialism is a satisfactory alternative to the present state of affairs.

There is, of course, no easy way of doing this. Even assuming that it is possible to know much about the effects of a reform before it has been tested on a large scale, it is hardly the easiest thing to know whether the net benefit (evil) from one social order outweighs the net benefit (evil) from another. One reason for this is that it is next to impossible to even determine whether a given social order produces a net gain or a net loss. It is extremely hard to quantify many of the effects of a social system — e.g., the alienation, anomie, and/or contentment to which it gives rise. Likewise, because of differences over moral values, over how to rank them or over whether a particular step will be conducive to the realization of shared values, people might differ as to whether or not a given effect of an institution is an evil or a good. For example, militant students who want the *status quo* overturned immediately and who rate this highest on their scale of values will not have much respect for a university that turns out thinking men and women who nonetheless are content to work for slow and peaceful reform. On the other hand, persons who, though feeling some distaste for the present social order aver that the good life is one featured by interest in things intellectual will be likely to consider that university a blessing to be preserved at almost all costs. The difference in the assessments of what the university is worth springs from the fact that the value most important to one judge is at best secondary to the other, and *vice versa*. But even with all these methodological obstacles in my way, I feel that I am morally obligated to make a conclusion of some sort as to whether decentralist socialism is a satisfactory alternative to the *status quo*. I shall weigh its potential merits against its potential demerits, take into account the probability or lack of such that these benefits and evils would in fact ensue, and then make a very rough judgment as to whether the new arrangements would be worthwhile in themselves and more acceptable than the socio-economic system that is ours at present. If decentralist socialism would be, on balance, productive of net harm or if it were only slightly preferable to welfare state capitalism, we would, of course, be justified in refusing to call it an adequate alternative. Our duty, then, would be to propose a third possibility that promised much more than its rival — though there is no room in this book to explain or defend such an alternative in any detail.

We have found that most existing institutions of participatory democracy have not in fact made those who select their personnel self-governing as to the issues with which they deal. We did see that some of the causes for failure of these organs are far from universal or are, at least, easily remediable. But other factors which experience and common sense show us prevent the average man from taking advantage of the creation of these bodies to convince his representatives thereon to vote as he wishes are much more difficult to eradicate in the near future. The reference here, of course, is to the fact that they are liable to become involved in discussing questions of little intrinsic importance; while he for his part will be a busy person with little time or energy to give to them and will worry a lot more about his family and personal problems than about any issue, significant or trivial, they decide to deal with. Also, the very fact that there is such a great number of potential obstacles to the goal of his becoming self-governing as a result of the implementation of participatory democracy should itself give those who believe decentralist socialism will be likely to accomplish this end some sobering second thoughts.

We also saw some dangerous "side-effects" which might result from the adoption of the ideas of the anti-bureaucratic radicals. Disregard for fundamental liberties, contempt for the legitimate needs of the larger political entity, excessive parochialism, a refusal to recognize the justifiable interests of the producer (or the consumer), the stirring up of race hatred or the prevention of racial integration, and a decline in the efficiency and/or the quality of certain services, might spring from the transfer of a great amount of decision-making power to neighborhood legislatures and factory works councils. However, we did note some devices for making the development of all these side-effects except the last-mentioned less likely. There are also we saw, some desirable by-products which might come from participatory democracy, such as the emergence of groups which might engage in interesting social experiments on a small scale and the development of agencies which are more likely to be responsive to intelligent suggestions from lower echelon employees than are the vast city, state and federal bureaucracies of today.

In sum, then, it does not seem very likely that the implementation of participatory democracy will get the average man to have much more say as an individual over the formation of the policy which affects his life than he has now. That is, it is not likely to make most men more self-governing; and it might, though we could to a large extent prevent this, lead to an increase in the suspicion, hatred, exploitation and inefficiency that plague the world today. But a fair treatment of the probable balance sheet of participatory democracy requires us to discuss here two or three more of its possible advantages.

One as yet unmentioned boon that would almost certainly spring from decentralist socialism is really twofold: it would make *some* persons self-governing who otherwise would not have been so and it would provide a training in the art of government for many of these persons. On the first point, those who are elected to the various community policy-making bodies plus those ordinary members of the community who pressure them to vote in one way or another would be exercising decision-making power in an area or areas from which their voices had been excluded in the past. The members of the local boards of education, for example, would be, overwhelmingly, individuals who had previously had no say whatsoever in formulating education policy. Likewise, a few members of the community who had been afraid to contact the central board of education about school problems (or who had no idea what agency controlled the schools) would doubtlessly get in touch with one or several of the members of the local board to try to influence them on some matter or other. There is no contradiction here between this and our conclusion in the last paragraph: we are not asserting here that participatory democracy would make the *majority* of persons (i.e., the average man) self-governing with respect to the issues with which the local policy-making bodies would deal; but merely that it would insure that a formerly impotent minority of the workers in a factory and of the residents in a neighborhood would, as individuals, exercise some control over the resolution of these questions. Thus decentralization of a city's school system would not produce a situation in which most men and women actually have a voice in the drafting of education policy; but it would probably increase the absolute number of the persons who do have such a voice.

On point two, there can be little doubt that the persons who are selected for the neighborhood boards and the factory works councils will be given an insight into the nature of politics and obtain an appreciation of how one can get at least some of his views transformed into binding rules that they otherwise would not have had. For example, the members of a community school board will learn that the community is financially dependent upon the larger society, that the persons they employ, no matter how committed to the goals of the board they seem at first, will soon be making demands of their own, that it will be impossible for them to supervise the day-to-day workings of the schools, and thus that it is inevitable that they will have to delegate a good deal of decision-making power to the men they hire to administer the schools. They will soon also be made aware that they knew little about some of the problems which they will have to resolve, and that in these matters, too, they will have to defer somewhat to the wisdom (or stupidity) of the professional (teacher, psychologist, principal, architect, engineer). They will also discover that some of their colleagues on the board will make proposals which they will want to reject but that they will have to accede to some extent to the wishes of these men if they want to get any of their own ideas accepted. In short, the members of the neighborhood boards and works councils will soon have it made crystal clear to them that there are significant limits on their powers and capacities and that to get anything of value done they will have to compromise; i.e., to permit other things to be done which they dislike. These talents, which let us reiterate, would be acquired by only a minority of individuals even under decentralist socialism (albeit a more sizeable minority than possesses them now), should enable these men not only to do something for their community in their role as members or constituents of the local legislature, but also to contribute something of benefit to the larger polity when and if they are "graduated" to membership on policy-making bodies having jurisdiction over the city, region or nation. As the sociologist Nathan Glazer has put it in an assessment of the Community Action agencies set up in the United States under the War on Poverty: "The agencies have provided a training ground for large numbers of local black community leaders, many of whom have become more militant, it is true, but many of whom are now on the first rungs of careers in electoral politics, and look forward to participating in the system as democratically elected representatives of citizens, rather than tearing it down."[1]

Proceeding with this description of certain additional benefits of participatory democracy, there are certain broad problems whose ramifications, nonetheless, differ from region to region or from street to street. In the United States, for example, there is a great deal of poverty, but the conditions of even the least affluent vary considerably. In the big city, the ghetto Negro is beset by crimes, drug addiction, lack of heat in winter, and the fear of starvation unless he gets his welfare check. But it is easy for him to get to a school or a library or buy a paper and sometimes simple for him to get to work. The Negro in the rural American south, on the other hand, lives in a relatively warm area, grows some of his own food, and is less plagued by the violence of his neighbors (though his father may have been beaten by Ku Klux Klan sympathizers). However, he may live miles from a school, store, or factory. The point is not that the southern Negro is better or worse off than the northern ghetto Negro; but merely that though both frequently are poor, the way in which they are affected by the blight of poverty is quite dissimilar. Therefore, the remedy for their troubles should vary, at least to some extent; and, more broadly, what ought to be done to solve a problem in area or neighborhood A may vary from what should be done in area or neighborhood B. It may be, for example, that neighborhood A needs an extension of a bus line so that its residents will be able to get to a factory which is offering them decent jobs; while what is demanded first of all in B is a vocational training program so that at least some of its inhabitants will be able to qualify for a skilled blue-collar position. And who knows best what is most needed in a neighborhood? To some extent, at least, the residents of the neighborhood! Who knows best what is needed at Harvard? Its students and faculty, of course! And it would be another happy by-product of participatory democracy that once it had been implemented, those who would be formulating policy for a given area or institution would be those most likely to know most about that area, etc. Thus, under participatory democracy, the residents of Harlem and their elective representatives would be formulating many of the rules which would apply in that community; the workers of the Ford plant in Dagenham, England, plus their elective works council would be operating that factory; and the students and faculty of the Free University of Berlin would be running that institution of higher learning!

Therefore decentralist socialism will make a few people more self-governing as individuals than at present; will teach a few who would not otherwise have learned how to govern wisely and well; and will insure that those who make the laws know something about the institution or territory for which they are legislating. Moreover, the achievement of these goals will be of real value, though we should discuss in some depth the extent of the urgency of the realization of the first-mentioned. Consequently, in adding up the accounts of participatory democracy we must recognize not only that these benefits *could* flow from the new system but that the odds are that they *would* spring from it. It is not as clear, however, that participatory democracy will produce "community", at least the sort of "community" that is needed in the present world. The reason we must inquire into this problem is that, to many anti-bureaucratic radicals, community is as important a product of participatory democracy as is increased self-government.[2] To quote again one of the lines of the Port Huron statement of the Students for a Democratic Society, "Loneliness, estrangement, isolation describe the vast distance between man today;" [3] and it is one of the main hopes of the authors of that essay that the new social order which they favor will lead to the replacement of this universal estrangement and isolation by "personal links between man and man. . . . , especially to go beyond the partial and fragmentary bonds of function that bind men only as worker to worker, employer to employee, teacher to student, American to Russian."[4] (G. D. H. Cole, as well, had a similar analysis of modern society. "But in the vast majority of streets there is not even the shadow of a social unity, joining these people together on the basis of their common neighborhood."[5] And, just as does the American SDS, this British Guild Socialist thought that one of the most important results of the creation of small neighborhood political units would be an increase in human comradeship.)

Just how is the establishment of a decentralist form of socialism supposed to bring about an increase in human brotherhood? The obvious way is this: if groups of neighbors (or workers) get together and discuss issues of common concern to them and which they have some power to resolve, either directly or through a neighborhood (factory) legislature which is highly responsive to their wishes, their discussion of politics will soon turn to a discussion of other, more personal matters, and so their relationship will soon be transformed from one of voter and voter to one of friend and friend. As the Port Huron Statement contends, one of the "root principles" underlying political life in a participatory democracy would be "that politics has the function of bringing people out of isolation and into community, thus being a necessary, though not sufficient, means of finding meaning in personal life".[6]

To determine whether participatory democracy is likely in fact to give rise to an increase in community we must, therefore, try to determine whether "political" dialogue between persons working in the same enterprise or living in the same locality who would otherwise not have come together is likely to lead to friendship. That is, will discussion of the impersonal soon transform itself into a relationship that is personal — and more than superficially so? Unfortunately, there is little evidence one way or the other. It would seem, though, that it *is* likely that some of the participants in the political debate will become friendly with some of the others who join in. Most of us do frequently see people whose initial relationship to us is impersonal, e.g., workmates, students, teachers, church members, and even bosses. However, we must not overemphasize the extent of the breakdown of "alienation of man frrom man" that will take place as a result of participatory democracy. One assumption of those who make this contention is that most of the community will participate in the dialogue about how the neighborhood or factory should resolve the issues facing it; as we have already seen, this may well not be the case. Just as important, (and what we have to say here is more relevant to the neighborhood than to the workplace), a discussion of issues such as how the schools ought to be run, whether the police should be more active in the enforcement of the laws against drugs, prostitution and gambling, etc. may reveal profound differences between persons in their approach to life. It may show Jones, a liberal who believes in freedom of expression and in allowing one to do that which will not hurt others, that his neighbor Smith, with whom he has been exchanging amicable but meaningless comments over the garden fence during the past five years, is a puritanical conservative who believes that gambling laws should be enforced rigorously and that books containing four-letter words or dealing with any controversial matter should be tossed out of school libraries and curricula. The superficial relations between Jones and Smith will be changed into a deeper one, it is true, but into one based on hatred, fear and contempt rather than upon mutual trust and understanding. Jones will start despising Smith as an authoritarian prude with quasi-fascist tendencies; while Smith will refer to Jones with disgust as a liberal do-gooder who fiddles while the moral fibre of our youth is weakened. Of course, persons with profound political differences *can* grow to respect rather than to dislike one another; but it is highly doubtful that this respect, which is essentially an intellectual thing, will ever ripen into true friendship.[7]

Also, one wonders whether the above-quoted contention of the SDS's Port Huron Statement that "loneliness, estrangement, isolation describe the vast distance between man today" is completely accurate. Even in the large city, most people do have friends. It is true that these friends often live in a different neighborhood or even in a suburb; but, thanks to the subway, bus and automobile, there is nothing so tragic about this. Thus it is arguable that even if participatory democracy does produce "community" in the neighborhood, it is giving rise to something that is not really needed under modern conditions. Of course, the advocates of participatory democracy would then retort that even in the case of one who had friends elsewhere, participatory democracy would still be valuable because in breaking down the barriers between him and his neighbors it would be increasing the number of his friendships. There is considerable validity in this retort, it must be admitted, but it overlooks one point. (Once again, what follows is not relevant to the factory.) If one surveys the conflicts that threaten the world most today, quarrels among neighbors will not be found. The most ominous antagonisms, at least on an intra-national level, involve clashes between racial and religious groups. The hatred between white and black in the United States is only the most obvious example: to this list can be added the clash between white and coloured in Great Britain, between Fleming and Walloon in Belgium, between black and Asian in Kenya and Guyana and between Catholic and Protestant Irishman in Ulster. Now the best way to reduce these frictions is for the members of one group to develop affection for members of its antagonist. And the antagonist usually lives outside one's neighborhood: no white men live in Harlem and few blacks live outside the Negro ghetto; the Protestants live on Belfast's Shankill Road; the Catholics on its Falls Road. Now it is, of course, completely foreign to the whole spirit of e.g., the Port Huron Statement to say that the individual who develops close ties in his home area as the result of participatory democracy should not bother to develop friendship in other communities. And, yet, there is the danger that just this would happen if participatory democracy became a reality; i.e., that the white Catholic who has become friendly with many other white Catholics in is predominantly Catholic neighborhood would feel it unnecessary or would not have the time to further his acquaintance with the Harlem Negro next to whom he works at the office. We saw in a previous chapter that the policy-making bodies of a neighborhood may well find it politically profitable to engage in racial discrimination or at least to refuse to take positive steps to increase the contacts between the ethnic group which is predominant in its area and others. (What has preceded in this paragraph serves, of course, as another policy argument on behalf of its taking such steps.) Similarly the sense of community in the neighborhood which the discussion of political issues by its residents might bring about might in turn reduce the already-too-sparse personal contacts between these residents and the inhabitants of another area populated by a different group. This in its stead would lessen the chance that the tension between the two groups could be amicably resolved. In addition, it would threaten the self-development of the individuals in the two areas, for one is more likely to grow mentally and spiritually when he comes in touch with ideas and/or life styles different from his own. The reader should refer again to the finding of the United States Commission on Civil Rights which we quoted in Chapter VIII. Other well-known examples of how contact between persons of different ethnic groups is conducive to an increase in creativity, etc. are (1) the use by American white composers of themes in American Negro jazz and (2) the stimulus given to American social science by the influx of European refugees fleeing Hitler.

We have just seen that one of the fundamental assumptions of the anti-bureaucratic radicals, i.e., that the development of close bonds among neighbors is a desirable phenomenon, may need some modification even though it seems self-evidently true on first glance. The fact that one of the supposedly "obvious" premises of the participatory democrats is not one hundred percent valid suggests to us that we had better inquire into the validity of another crucial thesis of theirs: the doctrine that the average man today is powerless. If he is not powerless as an individual, it is not self-evidently imperative to create a socio-economic system specifically designed to give him power of this sort. That is, one of the great benefits that will hopefully be produced by a system of participatory democracy is, as we have seen, the transformation of the average man into a self-governing person, i.e., a person who determines his own fate by convincing his elected representatives to vote his way on issues of interest to him. Now, if he already has a fair amount of control over his own life, one of the major needs that decentralist socialism is supposed to fulfill is largely met; and thus one of the major arguments in favor of this form of socialism must be discarded even before inquiring empirically whether it would in fact be likely to achieve this aim.

One contending that the individual already has a good deal of hegemony over the way he lives would bring up points such as the following. Many of the decisions that one feels are important are made by small groups of three or four of which he is a member. For example, the family makes a large number of determinations which, though trivial in an absolute sense, are of the highest significance to its members. "What time do I have to be home tonight?", the teenage daughter asks. "Do we have to visit those bores in Brooklyn?", the husband queries. "Do I have to cook a fancy meal tonight or will all of you be satisfied with a TV dinner?", the mother wonders. Likewise the small group of intimate friends will choose whether to go to the movies, bowling, the ball game or the theatre, while the three or four men who share the office will resolve who shall run out for the coffee that week. These decisions are trivial in a way, but at the time they are made they are felt by the members of the group to be momentous. And in most western societies, at least, each member has a real voice in settling these problems. He may not win out, but at least his point of view will have been considered and he is more likely to emerge the victor the "next time." If mother's idea of visiting those bores in Brooklyn carries the day, father's suggestion that we all stay home and sleep is quite possibly the winner next Sunday. If teenaged son Joe's friends decide to play poker this Saturday rather than to go for a ride as he wishes, they will at least have listened to Joe and may well follow his proposal next week. And since, Joe, father, mother, and most people do effectively participate in resolving the many problems of weight to them that are handled by the "face-to-face" groups to which they belong, it could be argued that the view that the individual *qua* individual is unable to affect the course of his existence is quite a false one.

The point of view expressed in the above paragraph does have something to it; but there is even more to the decentralist socialists' position that for the most part the individual as individual does lack the power to control his own destiny.

(Ignored here will be the obvious fact that in any developed society with a division of labor we are dependent upon the knowledge of others — e.g., the ability of the auto mechanic to diagnose what is wrong with the car and to set matters right.)

It is true that father's office group may be able to determine who gets the coffee that week; but father alone has little or no say about fixing the hours he works or even choosing whether he will keep his job. Joe might be able to convince the boys to take a drive, but he alone will not be able to convince the Congress of the United States that military conscription is immoral or even to get the mayor and Parks Commissioner to agree that the city should build and maintain a big lot for teenagers who want to do some auto racing. In other words, the individual acting alone may be able to shape certain decisions which touch his life, but he has little or no say over the resolution of those which are really important. (That Joe may think that where he goes on Saturday is more significant than whether he has to register for the draft is not pertinent for our purposes: if he holds this view he will be likely to remain content with the political *status quo;* but he will still be helpless.) We are not asserting here, of course, that we ought to implement decentralist socialism because it will give the impotent mass man some influence: as even the most casual reader will be aware by now, the arguments pro and con participatory democracy are numerous and complex and it would probably be a failure in this respect anyhow. But to reject it on the ground that the individual does have a good deal of power over his life at present would be unfortunate because then its condemnation would rest upon a premise that is largely, though not wholly, false.

The last point that should be noted in toting up the benefits and weaknesses of participatory democracy is that certain advantages this system would obviously have it would share with *any* polity which featured free elections in which each man's vote counted equally, i.e., in which the principle of the rule of the numerical majority prevailed. The elections for neighborhood legislature would induce the voters to think about the questions involved and to develop as moral beings by campaigning and voting for the candidate with the most satisfactory position on these matters. However, issues such as these (e.g., education, recreational facilities) are at present usually involved in citywide elections, and there is no reason to believe that these citywide elections have less potential for being a stimulus of this sort. The neighborhood legislators, as we have seen, would have to pay some attention to public opinion since it is the people who would decide whether to retain them in office, but as we have already noted, so must, e.g., a city council, and for just the same reason. Those whom the laws affect would have a chance to give their verdict on them if decentralist socialism were to come into being; but the citizens of a city in a democratic nation can even now protest against or praise that town's legislation and vote against or for its policymakers. In short, the classic arguments in favor of political democracy justify free elections on a one-man one-vote basis generally, but cannot be used to prove that certain matters should be resolved by a smaller rather than by a larger unit. Likewise, these arguments can be used to back up the thesis that workers (students) should be given some say in the management of their factories (colleges); but they do not really help us answer the question of whether all the workers (students) in the nation should be considered as one unit and elect one set of representatives to help formulate policy applicable to all the country's factories (universities) or whether, on the other hand, the workers (students) in each plant (college) should pick representatives for the purpose of formulating rules applicable to that institution alone. They also support the proposition that the consumers ought to have a say in the running of retail stores; but they do not help us with the problem of whether every adult in the country should select a body of representatives whose functions would be to help promulgate broad retail store policy or whether the comparatively small group that shops in the local supermarket should have the power to control that particular supermarket. Speaking more abstractly again, they back up the position of those who favor popular control over law-making; but have little or no relevance to the important problems of whether "the people" should be considered as united into one group or divided into many groups for the p:rpose of formulating policy, and, if the latter, of how extensive each of these groups should be. (Analogously, almost everyone in the United States before the Civil War believed that the United States Constitution was the product of the will of the people. This mutual belief, however, did not prevent a bitter quarrel between North and South about whether "the people" meant "the people as a whole" or "the people divided into the populations of the thirteen original states.")

We can finally come to a reluctant and highly tentative conclusion about the desirability of "decentralist socialism". To repeat, it is not likely to achieve one of the two most cherished goals of its supporters, i.e., the creation of a citizen body the majority of whose members are self-governing. We have also given reasons why it might not produce more "community" (the other fundamental value of its adherents.) We have indicated that there is some doubt whether there is as much need for an expansion of "community" as the decentralist socialists maintain, and that the sort of "community" which it is most likely to further, the tie between like and like, may threaten the growth of bonds between unlike—the links the world needs most today. There is, too, the problem of controlling the tendency towards the preservation of the segregated status quo, the neglect of the national welfare, the disregard of the consumer's or producer's interest, the inefficiency, and even the tyranny of the small groups of which it would be comprised. Though these effects to some extent could be prevented, and though decentralist socialism would facilitate social experimentation, train a few additional persons in the art of good government, and keep those ignorant of a locality from setting rules for it, we are forced to conclude that, as a social order, it would be of insignificant net utility.

It would be, therefore, an *unsatisfactory* alternative to the welfare state capitalism of today. The numerous weaknesses of welfare state capitalism are documented in numerous books and readers on both domestic and foreign policy and, therefore, there is no need to repeat them here. However, we know it, and the majority of people in the Western world are fairly comfortable with it, and so it seems a bit useless to replace it with another system of which we also must say that its benefits could add up to not much more than its detriments. To put this in another way, it would be a waste of effort to escape the harsh New York winters by taking a trip to slightly more temperate Philadelphia! (Admittedly, one could infer from what has appeared in this book not the above mentioned conclusion but one to the effect that participatory democracy would be very desirable. One who made such an inference would be one struck by, e.g., the potential of the system for trying out particular social changes on a small scale and the relative ease with which the nation as a whole can take steps to insure that the small units into which it is divided will not sabotage the general welfare.)

But a sense of duty prevents us from closing here. As a social scientist I can conclude by saying that decentralist socialism would be only a slight improvement over the capitalism of today; but as a social and political theorist and a man it is at least my obligation to say whether I think that there is a social system significantly more desirable than the one with which we have at present.

I believe that there is, and that this alternative is what can be termed a liberal, democratic but moderately centralized socialism. (Obviously the alternative, at least for the West, is not any of the political systems that are presently called communist. The dearth of political liberty that seems to have become a concomitant of this sort of state makes even American capitalism seem infinitely preferable.) Now it is not my main purpose in this book to defend centralized socialism against capitalism and decentralist socialism, and thus my statement on behalf of it will be brief indeed. However, as state socialism is very much on the defensive today, and as there is absolutely no reason for the reader to accept the bald statement that it (combined with political democracy), is the best form of government for the West in this day and age, I must devote at least a couple of paragraphs to noting the most generally accepted arguments in favor of it.

Under centralist socialism, the central government will own and manage the major units of the economy. The great advantage of this over capitalism is, as any orthodox socialist would contend, that these units will be operated for the benefit of the nation as a whole rather than for the profit of the owners. And, as differentiated from what would happen under participatory democracy, what the nation's major concerns produce, what prices they charge, what machinery is to be used, etc. would be determined by high-ranking officials of the central government and not by factory works councils or consumers organizations, so that the wants, needs and desires of the whole nation with respect to these matters could be adequately satisfied. Moreover, under participatory democracy, there would be a preference for small factories and small stores, as these are easiest for factory, consumers, and neighborhood councils to control. The centralized socialist state would be more willing to set up large factories and stores, when these are necessary to take advantage of economies of size. It would also be more able to insure that the various sorts of business establishments are rationally, located, taking into account, for example, the need of workers to be near their jobs, of an enterprise to be near its markets, of consumers having at least one store in their city where they can buy a specialized product they want, of residential areas to be free of traffics and pollution, etc.

Under centralist socialism also, the national government would be charged with the task of ending poverty and unemployment. This would be the most certain way of insuring that all residents of the country were free from economic worries and that lesser political units (including neighborhood governments) did not keep levels of relief low as a device for keeping poor people out of the area. Instead of transferring powers from city to neighborhood, centralist socialism would fuse the city with its surrounding metropolitan areas so as to make use of economies of size, to facilitate contact among peoples of various ethnic backgrounds, and to bring about increased specialization and cooperation in the areas of education, culture, recreation, air and water pollution control, fire, police, transport, health, etc.

In short, centralist socialism is a better device than participatory democracy for insuring the realization of three of my basic values: the provision of a decent standard living for all, the efficient use of scarce resources, and the lessening of racial tension. But it is also extremely important to me that the individual who wants this have some say as an individual in making the policy that affects his life; that there be room in society for flexibility and experimentation; and that groups who desperately desire a particular reform be able to obtain it if granting it to them will not threaten the welfare of the country as a whole. Therefore centralist socialism should make use of several of the ideas of the participatory democrats, ideas which, if put into practice, might help achieve one or more of the goals mentioned in the last sentence. It should create works councils in each factory with limited power over working conditions, plant facilities, vacations, etc. It should encourage the development of some small consumers and producers cooperatives as well as (and the decentralist socialist might well demur here) of some small, privately owned profit-making enterprises, justifying the latter on the ground that there should always be a place for the man who hates to be bossed. It should allow educational institutions a considerable amount of autonomy: we are so far from knowing what sort of education is good for what sort of person that more and yet more experimentation is needed in this area. It should require each government bureau or public corporation that performs a given service to consult with an advisory council composed of a representative sample of consumers of that service and encourage consumers to articulate their complaints about that bureau, etc. It should allow neighborhoods, a majority of whose residents feel themselves totally outside the present social order, some control over certain institutions serving the neighborhood (simultaneously using the courts, etc. to insure that these neighborhoods do not abuse their powers and that the institutions are managed efficiently and that their activities are coordinated with those of similar institutions in other areas). The benefit of this would be, as Altshuler mentions with specific reference to black control of black communities, that "it would give blacks a tangible stake in the American political system. By giving them systems they considered their own, it would hopefully enhance the legitimacy of the whole system in their eyes."[8] Also, if the residents of a neighborhood or the workers in a factory enthusiastically want control over neighborhood or factory governance, it would be a threat to the stability of the social order *not* to give them a certain portion of what they want, once again under conditions that will prevent them from misusing their new-found authority. "Law and order" may not be the noblest end of government, but it is fundamental nonetheless, and political systems should be willing to make certain concessions in order to preserve it. It is doubtful that even the incorporation into a centralist socialist state of all the "decentralist" reforms noted in this paragraph would transform it into a participatory democracy, for major policy would continue to be made at the center (or at the regional or metropolitan level in some instances) by democratically elected public officials and their appointees. However, there is no clear line demarcating the boundary between centralist socialism and decentralist socialism, and if a reader wishes to label "participatory democracy" what we are calling "centralist socialism with an admixture of decentralist socialism", he should feel free to do so.

Two more points must be made now. We have not said much so far about violent sit-ins, destruction of property, disruptions of classrooms and speakers, seizure of college buildings by armed militants, bombings of electric power stations and all the other tactics employed by some in the amorphous group we are calling the participatory democrats. The reason for this omission is that there is nothing in the theory of decentralist socialism that demands that it be realized by force and violence. A decentralist socialist is free to argue, and many do argue, that the ballot box and (perhaps) nonviolent civil disobedience are the only strategies that should be employed to achieve his goals. To have emphasized that some decentralist socialists believe that violent confrontations are justified because these and similar devices are the only way they can make the public conscious of their views would have been to have prejudiced many readers *ab initio* against decentralist socialism and thus to have prevented them from following objectively the arguments con and pro its political philosophy that have appeared in this book.

A word now about decentralist socialism and the future. It is arguable that the Marxists are right in asserting the primacy of the economic over the political and that changes in technology will have more influence on the future of the globe than alterations in the political system. In any event, it is quite possible that in fifty or seventy five years the life style of the 1970's will have completely disappeared and we shall be living in a heavily automated world. Though men will still be far from perfect, we could well have, at least in the western world, a society in which some of the visions of Karl Marx and Edward Bellamy are economically practicable.

On the one hand, not only could poverty be banished from the land; but payment according to what one needs could be the rule. On the other hand, the average man would only have to work a couple of hours a day in order for his bounteous harvest of goods and services to be ripe for plucking by the consumer. Assuming that some sort of socialism (i.e., public ownership of the means of consumption and distribution) will prevail in 2040, which type of socialism would be more appropriate for such a society, centralist or decentralist?

Even in this new era centralized socialism should still hold sway. To insure the fabrication of all the commodities that will have to be produced in order that a high level of consumption for each individual be attained, and to insure that this production requires only a few hours work from each citizen, the individual enterprises will have to be huge and what is done in one firm will have to be rigorously correlated with what is done in the others so that there is little or no waste of scarce factors of production. Real workers' control of a huge plant is difficult to maintain, and, in any case, the required coordination would of itself deprive the decision-makers located in the several plants of a great deal of autonomy. Thus to this extent decentralist socialism would be impracticable in the society of the future.

Moreover, in this society transport and communications should be so advanced over what they are now that by means of a ten cent phone call we should be able to not only hear but to see on a "phonevision" screen anyone in the world and should be able to be by his side in a matter of a few hours at cheap prices. In such a world, emphasis on the neighborhood, to say nothing of the nation-state, would seem at first totally irrelevant. On the other hand, men and women will have almost the whole day to themselves in this society; and there is the great danger that out of sheer boredom they might wreck the complex and ingenious world they have created. Thus it is at least arguable that each neighborhood should be permitted in this society of 2040 A.D. to maintain and operate certain educational, recreational and social facilities for its residents so that they will be able to spend their almost endless leisure hours harmlessly if not constructively. Not that everyone in this society would spend most of his time in the neighborhood: in fact it could be anticipated that most people will spend much of their new-found leisure in other neighborhoods, cities and even countries. But even in this "science fiction" world the concept of the neighborhood government should not be totally discarded, for its performance of a few modest functions such as those described above may keep the more populous and more sophisticated society which will flourish above it from being drowned in a bloodbath initiated by bored men and women looking for "kicks." More than this cannot be claimed for it; but if it could succeed in this aim its contribution to the human life of the twenty-first century would indeed be invaluable.[9]

FOOTNOTES TO CHAPTER X

1. See his "For White and Black, Community Control is the Issue," *New York Times Magazine,* April 27, 1969, at p. 50. Alan Altshuler's *Community Control* agrees with the thesis that neighborhood government would get neighborhood leaders to see that the solution of urban problems is a difficult matter which cannot be solved by sloganeering or simple cure-alls. See p. 205.

2. In his influential *The Poverty of Liberalism,* (Boston: Beacon Paperbacks, 1969) Robert Paul Wolff calls "affective community" and "productive community" a phenomenon not too dissimilar from that which we are labelling "community." And what we are calling a "citizen body whose members are self governing," he refers to as a "rational community". See his Chapter 5, especially p. 192.

3. Jacobs and Landau, *The New Radicals,* p. 155.

4. *Ibid.,* p. 155.

5. See his *Essays in Social Theory* (paperback ed., London: Oldbourne, 1962) , at pp. 108-109.

6. Jacobs and Landau, *op. cit.,* p. 156.

7. Robert Nisbet, speaking of small groups in general, says that "from the viewpoint of social interaction, the small group can as easily heighten feelings of hatred or misery as it can feelings of friendship and mutual agreement." See p. 91 of *The Social Bond,* (New York: Knopf, 1970). Nisbet is an opponent of centralism. It is, of course, open to argument that true friendship is not a necessary ingredient of life. However, Eric Fromm contends, p. 36 of *The Sane Society,* that "The necessity to unite with other living beings, to be related to them, is an imperative need on the fulfillment of which man's sanity depends," and surely deep friendship is one of the most socially beneficial of such unions.

8. See p. 199 of *op. cit.*

9. Victor Ferkiss believes that in fact decisions about the complicated problems of the future may well be made on the same basis of private interest and the struggle between interest groups as they are made today. See his *Technological Man,* (New York: George Braziller, 1969) pp. 176-196

   I must confess that Murray Bookchin brilliantly argues that the most efficient economic unit of the future will be an enterprise that is so small that all its workers will be able to have some say in managing it. See his "Toward a Liberatory Technology", pp. 96, ff. of Benello and Roussopolous (eds.), *The Case for Participatory Democracy.*

Selected Bibliography

I. Works By or About the Intellectual Precursors of the Current Call for Participatory Democracy

Beer, Max. *A History of English Socialism*. Vol. II. London: G. Bell and Sons, 1920.

Bakunin, Michael. "Letters to the Comrades of the International Workingmen's Association of Locle and Chaux-de-Fonds." In *Socialist Thought*, edited by Albert Fried and Ronald Sanders, p. 332ff. New York: Doubleday Anchor, 1964.

Blanc, Louis. "Organization of Labor." In Fried and Sanders, *op. cit.*, p. 230ff.

Cole, George Douglas Howard. *The Case for Industrial Partnership*. London: Macmillan, 1957.

——. *Essays in Social Theory*. London: Oldbourne Book Co., 1962

——. *Fabian Socialism*. London: George Allen and Unwin, 1964.

——. *Guild Socialism Restated*. London: Leonard Parsons, 1921.

——. *History of Socialist Thought*. 5 vols. London: Macmillan, 1953-60.

——. *National Coal Board*. London: Gollancz, n.d.

——. "Post-Stalinist Shock." *Nation* 183:90, August 4, 1956.

——. *Self-Government in Industry*. 5th ed. revised. London: G. Bell and Sons, 1920.

——. *Social Theory*. London: Methuen and Co., 1920.

——. *Workers' Control and Self-Government in Industry*. London: Gollancz, 1933.

Fourier, Charles. "Selections." In Fried and Sanders, *op. cit.*, p. 142ff.

Hobson, Samuel G. "An Interlude with Mr. Cole." *New Age* 22:286, Feb. 7, 1918.

————. "Nation, State and Government." *New Age* 23:5, May 2, 1918.

————. *National Guilds.* 2nd ed. London: G. Bell and Sons, 1917.

Jefferson, Thomas. "Letter to Samuel Kercheval." Excerpted in *Free Government in the Making,* by Alpheus T. Mason, p. 369ff. New York: Oxford University Press, 1949.

Kropotkin, Peter. *Mutual Aid.* Boston: Porter Sargent, n.d.

Laidler, Harry. *Social-Economic Movements.* New York: Thomas Y. Crowell, 1949.

Lenin, V. I. "State and Revolution." In *Essential Works of Marxism,* edited by Arthur P. Mendel, p. 103ff. New York: Bantam Books, 1961.

Marx, Karl. "The Civil War in France." In *Marx and Engels,* edited by Lewis S. Feuer, p. 362ff. New York: Doubleday, 1959.

————. "Economic and Philosophical Manuscripts." In *Karl Marx: Early Writings,* translated and edited by T. B. Bottomore, p. 63ff. New York: McGraw Hill, 1964.

Marx, Karl and Friedrich. "The Communist Manifesto." In Mendel, *op. cit.,* p. 13ff.

Owen, Robert, *A New View of Society and Other Writings.* London: J. M. Dent and Sons, 1927.

Proudhon, Pierre J. *What is Property?* New York: Dover, 1970.

Taft, Philip. *Movements for Economic Reform.* New York: Rinehart and Co., 1950.

II. The Theory of Participatory Democracy: Advocacy, Criticism and Exposition

Altshuler, Alan. *Community Control.* New York: Pegasus, 1970.

Benello, C. George and Dmitrios Roussopolous, eds. *The Case for Participatory Democracy.* New York: Grossman, 1971.

Bookchin, Murray. "Post-Scarcity Anarchy." In *American Radical Thought: The Libertarian Tradition,* edited by Henry Silberman, p. 321. Lexington, Mass.: D.C. Heath, 1970.

————. "Toward a Liberatory Technology." In Benello and Roussopolous, *op. cit.,* p. 96ff.

Carmichael, Stokely and Charles Hamilton. *Black Power.* New York: Vintage, 1967.

Cohn-Bendit, Daniel, et. al. *The French Student Revolt: The Leaders Speak.* New York: Hill and Wang, 1968.

Cook, Terence and Patrick Morgan, eds. *Participatory Democracy*. San Francisco: Canfield Press, 1971.

Glazer, Nathan. "For White and Black, Community Control is the Issue." *New York Times Magazine,* April 27, 1969, p. 34ff.

Goodman, Paul. *Growing Up Absurd*. New York: Random House, 1960.

————. *People or Personnel*. New York: Random House, 1963.

Hamilton, Charles. "An Advocate of Black Power Defines It." *New York Times Magazine,* April 14, 1968, p. 22ff.

Hayden, Tom. "At Issue: Peaceful Change or Civil War." *New York Times,* March 9, 1971, p. 37.

Jacobs, Paul and Saul Landau, eds. *The New Radicals*. New York: Random House Vintage Books, 1966.

Long, Priscilla, ed. *The New Left*. Boston: Porter Sargent, 1969.

Mailer, Norman. "Why Are We in New York?" *New York Times Magazine,* May 18, 1969, p. 101ff.

Mullen, William F. "Community Control and Black Political Participation." In Cook and Morgan, *op. cit.,* p. 256ff.

Oglesby, Carl. "Two Issues Revised." In Silberman, *op. cit.,* p. 348ff.

Pranger, Robert. *The Eclipse of Citizenship*. New York: Holt, Rinehart and Winston, 1968.

Reich, Charles. *The Greening of America*. New York: Bantam Books, 1971.

————. "Issues for a New Society." *New York Times,* March 9, 1971, p. 37.

Rustin, Bayard. "The Failure of Black Separatism." In Cook and Morgan, *op. cit.,* p. 280ff.

Savio, Mario. "Speech on the Steps of the University of California at Berkeley Administration Building." In Jacobs and Landau, *op. cit.,* p. 230ff.

Teodori, Massimo, ed. *The New Left: A Documentary History*. Indianapolis: Bobbs-Merrill, 1969.

Wolff, Robert Paul. *The Poverty of Liberalism*. Boston: Beacon Press, 1969.

III. Workers' Control of Industry in Practice

Adizes, Ichak. *Industrial Democracy: Yugoslav Style*. New York: Free Press, 1971.

Babeau, André. *Les Conseils Ouvriers en Pologne*. Paris: Librarie Armand-Colin, 1960.

Bussey, llene. "Management and Labor in West Germany." *Monthly Labor Review,* August 1970, p. 28.

Clagg, Hugh. *A New Approach to Industrial Democracy.* Oxford: Basil Blackwell, 1963.

Dragnich, Alex. *Tito's Promised Land.* New Brunswick: Rutgers University Press, 1954.

Klein, Alfons. *Mitbestimmung-Betriebsverfasssung-Personalvertretung.* Stuttgart: M. Kohlhammer Verlag, 1962.

Kolaja, Jiri. *A Polish Factory.* Lexington, Kentucky: University of Kentucky Press, 1960.

————. "A Yugoslav Workers' Coucil." *Human Organization* 20:27, Spring, 1961.

Loucks, W. N. "Workers' Self-Government in Yugoslav Industry." *World Politics* 11:68, October, 1958.

Neal, Fred W. *Titoism in Action.* Berkeley: University of California Press, 1958.

————. "Workers' Management of Industry in Yugoslavia." *American Universities Field Staff Reports,* S. E. European Series, Vol. 2, #3, 1954, p. 4.

Neuloh, Otto. *Der Neue Betriebsstil.* Tübingen: B. Mohr, 1960.

New York Times, Jan. 9, 1962, p. 54; April 25, 1962, p. 7.

Obradovic, Josip, John R. P. French, Jr. and Willard Rodgers. "Workers' Councils in Yugoslavia." *Human Relations* 23:459, Oct. 1970.

Potthoff, Eric, Otto Blume and Helmut Duvernell. *Zwischenbilanz der Mitbestimmung.* Tübingen: J. C. B. Mohr (Paul Siebeck), 1962.

Presidence du Conseil, Secretariat General du Gouvernement. *La Courte Expérience des Conseils Ouvriers en Pologne.* Paris: La Documentation Française, Notes et Études Documentaires, Aug. 26, 1958, #2453.

"Self Management with Tears." *The Economist,* Feb. 24, 1968, p. 40.

Spiro, H. J. *The Politics of German Codetermination.* Cambridge, Mass.: Harvard University Press, 1958.

Sturmthal, Adolf. *Workers' Councils.* Cambridge, Mass.: Harvard University Press, 1964.

Underwood, Paul. "Red Regime Cuts Yugoslav Wages." *New York Times,* August 19, 1962, p. 13.

Université Libre de Bruxelles, Institute de Sociologie Solvay, Centre d'Etude des Pays de l'est (ed.) *Le Régime et Les Institutions de la République Federative de Yugoslavie.* Brussels: Universite Libre de Bruxelles, 1959.

Wagner, Hardy R. H. *Erfahrungen mit dem Betriebsverfassungsgesetz.* Köln: Bund-Verlag GMBH, 1960.

IV. Descriptions of Workings of Neighborhood, Regional, and Educational Institutions of Self-Government

American Arbitration Association. *Representative Elections and Voter Participation in Community Action Programs Under OEO.* New York: American Arbitration Association, 1966.

"Answering the Dissidents: Civil Liberties in New York." New York: New York Civil Liberties Union, March 1969, p. 8.

Bell, Colin. "Scots Nationalism and the Heather Roots." *New Statesman* 75:754, June 7, 1968.

Clark, Kenneth B. and Jeannette Hopkins. *A Relevant War Against Poverty.* New York: Harper and Row, 1969.

Donovan, John. *The Politics of Poverty.* New York: Pegasus, 1967.

Dykes, Archie. *Faculty Participation in Academic Decision Making.* Washington: American Council on Education, 1968.

Kotler, Milton. *Neighborhood Government.* Indianapolis: Bobbs-Merrill, 1969.

Kramer, Ralph M. *Participation of the Poor.* Englewood Cliffs, New Jersey: Prentice Hall, 1969.

Mayer, Martin. "The Full and Sometimes Very Surprising Story of Ocean Hill, the Teachers Union and the Teacher Strikes of 1968." *New York Times Magazine,* Feb. 2, 1969, p. 18.

New York Times, Jan. 30, 1969, p. 7; April 29, 1969, p. 30; March 21, 1970, p. 30; March 28, 1970, p. 20; June 3, 1970, p. 53; Sept. 20, 1970, p. 43; Sept. 30, 1970, p. 2; Nov. 17, 1970, p. 1; Nov. 18, 1970, p. 42; March 29, 1971, p. 26; May 22, 1971, p. 25; June 12, 1971, p. 15; June 19, 1971, p. 1.

Scheibla, Shirley. *Poverty is Where the Money Is.* New Rochelle, New York: Arlington House, 1968.

"Where Were the Poor on Election Day?" *U.S. News and World Report,* March 21, 1966, p. 94.

Wilson, Frank L. "French-Canadian Separatism." *Western Political Quarterly* 20:116, March 1967.

V. Miscellaneous

Ferkiss, Victor. *Technological Man*. New York: George Braziller, 1969.

Fromm, Erich. *The Sane Society*. New York: Fawcett, 1965.

Heller, Walter. *New Dimensions of Political Economy*. Cambridge, Mass.: Harvard University Press, 1966.

Kahn, Herman. *On Thermonuclear War*. Princeton: Princeton University Press, 1961.

Kirk, Russell. *A Program for Conservatives*. Chicago: Regnery, 1962.

Lane, Robert. *Political Ideology*. New York: Free Press, 1962.

Lipset, Seymour. *Political Man*. New York: Doubleday Anchor, 1963.

Marcuse, Herbert, *One Dimensional Man*. Boston: Beacon Paperbacks, 1966.

Myrdal, Gunnar. *Beyond the Welfare State*. New York: Bantam Books, 1971.

New field, Jack. *A Prophetic Minority*. New York: New American Library, 1966.

Rosenberg, Morris. "Self Esteem and Concern with Public Affairs." *Public Opinion Quarterly* 26:201, Summer, 1962.

Stouffer, Samuel. *Communism, Conformity and Civil Liberties*. New York: Doubleday, 1955.

United States Commission on Civil Rights. *Racial Isolation in the Public Schools*. Washington: U. S. Government Printing Office, 1967.

INDEX

administrative agencies (see bureaucracy).

AFDCU program (U.S.), 188.

Almond, Gabriel and Verba, Sidney, 192.

Altshuler, Alan, 70n, 179n, 182n, 226.

American Arbitration Association, 96, 107-108n, 118-120.

American Civil Liberties Union (see also New York Civil Liberties Union), 152.

American Council on Education, 88, 91, 107n.

American Indians, 198.

anarchism, and relationship to participatory democracy, 22-24.

Ann Arbor, Mich., 140.

anti-bureaucratic radicalism [left, socialism] (see participatory democracy).

anti-consumer [producer] conduct (see overly anti-consumer [producer] conduct).

anti-poverty boards (see community action agencies).

anti-rationalism, current, causes of, 199-201; explanation for call for participatory democracy, 186, 198-201.

Babeau, Andre, 140n.

Bakunin, Mikhail, 23-24.

Belfast, Northern Ireland, 155, 217.

Belgium, 12, 127.

Bell, Colin, 19n.

Bellamy, Edward, 227.

Benello, C. George and Roussopolous, Dimitrios, 58n, 230n.

Berkeley, Calif., 61, 186.

Blanc, Louis, 23.

Bookchin, Murray, 58n, 62, 230n.

Boston, Mass., 96.

bourse du travail, 24.

Brandeis, Louis, 176.

Brittany, 16, 17, 197.

Brown v. Board of Education, 157.

bureaucrat, when self-governing citizen, 48-49.

bureaucracy, as possible control over participatory democracy, 167; participatory democracy as curing evils of, 178-79, 210; self-governing citizen and, 49-51.

Canada (see also Quebec), 190.

capitalism and private enter-

112; elections for, 83; employee interest in, 77, 82-83, 109, 114, 117; German (West), 74-76, 78-81, 82-83, 112, 115, 117, 146; legislation about, 74-76, 145, 167; obstacles to success, (see participatory democracy, obstacles to success); performance or non-performance of duties, 76, 77-81, 111-12, 114; personnel matters, 75-76, 79, 80, 81; plant personnel meeting, 81, 82, 83, 84; plant welfare matters, 75, 76, 79, 80, 81; Poland, 74, 83, 112-13; possible effects of (see prices and wages, *infra* and participatory democracy, possible effects of); prices, action on, 74, 145-46, 158-162, 167; production, determination of, 74; responsiveness to electorate, 77, 81-82, 109, 114, 115; self-governing citizen, creation of through works councils, 83; trivialities, discussion of, 125; vacations and hours of work, 75, 79, 80; wages, actions on, 75, 78, 79, 80, 81, 115, 148-50, 158-162, 167; Yugoslavian, 74-75, 76, 77-78, 81, 83, 112, 115, 125, 136, 138, 145-46, 148-50, 158-62, 167.

Yorty, Sam, 113, 114.

Yugoslavia, Communist Party of Yugoslavia, 112, 140n; works councils (see works councils, Yugoslavian).